SCOTTISH STEAM'S FINAL FLING

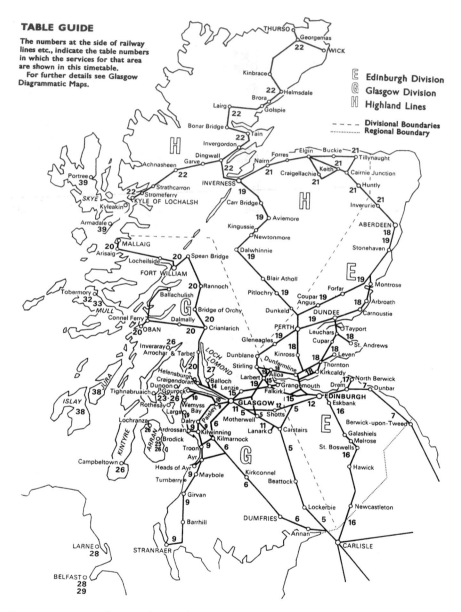

E Edinburgh Division
G Glasgow Division
H Highland Lines

– – – Divisional Boundaries
· · · · · Regional Boundary

System map extract from BR's Scottish Region 1966 timetable.

SCOTTISH STEAM'S FINAL FLING

EXTRACTS FROM A
TEENAGER'S
NOTEBOOKS

KEITH WIDDOWSON

The
History
Press

First published 2017

The History Press
The Mill, Brimscombe Port
Stroud, Gloucestershire, GL5 2QG
www.thehistorypress.co.uk

British Library Cataloguing in Publication Data.
A catalogue record for this book is available from the British Library.

ISBN 978 0 7509 7022 8

Typesetting and origination by The History Press
Printed and bound in Great Britain by TJ International Ltd

CONTENTS

ABOUT THE AUTHOR

Keith Widdowson was born, to his pharmacist father and secretarial mother, during the calamitous winter of 1947 at St Mary Cray, Kent, and attended the nearby schools of Poverest and Charterhouse. He joined British Railways in June 1962 as an enquiry clerk at the Waterloo telephone bureau – 'because his mother had noted his obsession with collecting timetables'.

Thus began a forty-five-year career within various train planning departments throughout BR, the bulk of which was at Waterloo but also included locations at Cannon Street, Wimbledon, Crewe, Euston, Blackfriars, Paddington and finally Croydon – specialising in dealing with train crew arrangements. After spending several years during the 1970s and '80s in Cheshire, London and Sittingbourne, he returned to his roots in 1985 where he finally met the steadying influence in his life, Joan, with whom he had a daughter, Victoria. In addition to membership of the local residents' association (St Pauls Cray), the Sittingbourne & Kemsley Light Railway and the U3A organisation, he keeps busy writing articles for railway magazines and gardening.

ACKNOWLEDGEMENTS

This book is dedicated to my ever-understanding wife Joan. Prior to meeting me many years ago the steam locomotive was an unknown subject to her. Having met many of my like-minded chasing friends when visiting preserved railways on their gala days, together with accompanying me on book signings, she has become resigned to the 'different' world I inhabit.

Then there is John Bird of Railway Images without whom the photographs accompanying this book would not have been of publishable quality. He has taken the negatives from all those years ago, squirrelled away in boxes and envelopes, and performed minor miracles. Thanks also to The History Press team without whom books, such as this, detailing my steam age travels, might never have seen the light of day.

Finally, many thanks to my lifelong friend and fellow traveller Graham 'Jock' Aitken who proofread this book.

INTRODUCTION

This, the fourth tome on my steam train travels during the mid 1960s, unlike two of its predecessors, cannot contain the word 'chase' in its title. Residing in Kent, I was never going to blitz Scotland to travel with as many different steam locomotives as was my self-imposed mission elsewhere in Britain – distance alone precluded such an activity. This book therefore is a personal travelogue of observations and experiences gained while undertaking my forays over the border during the final two years of Scottish steam (1965–67). Having said that, taking into consideration each visit started and finished with overnight services from England, at least I made full use of the hours there, undertaking the search-and-find pursuit necessary in order to track down the increasingly elusive steam passenger services.

Had I left it too late? What, steam wise, remained to be witnessed and travelled behind? Most of the express services over the WCML, so long the preserve of LMS Princess, Duchess, Patriot, Scot and Jubilee classes, were now in the hands of diesels. Likewise, the express services over the ECML, so long monopolised by Peppercorn's A1 and A2s together with Gresley's A3 and A4s, had also become devoid of steam. Admittedly a few of those LNER Pacifics had survived and, as I will recount in this book, were able to be caught working internal services within Scotland. As for tank locomotives, all the Fowler, Stanier, Johnson and former Caley representatives had long gone. Elsewhere the Great North of Scotland and West Highland lines had dispensed with steam many years earlier.

My interest in railway travels did not manifest itself within me until 1964. I was a 17-year-old junior BR clerk at the Waterloo-based Telephone Enquiry

Bureau of the Southern Region, and with the restricted funds available it was easier and financially cheaper to concentrate initially on travelling the routes throughout southern Britain threatened by the Beeching axe. Gradually my horizons expanded and with the ever-growing confidence associated with youth I embarked on my first Scottish trip in May 1965. The catalyst for this adventure was the imminent closure of the line between Dumfries and Stranraer – known colloquially as the Port Road. This was all new territory to a wide-eyed teenager and after having undertaken this initial jaunt over the border I vowed, when finances permitted, to return again. I was unaware of the paucity of steam on offer. There was no Internet-sourced information available to me – you had to go by word of mouth amongst fellow enthusiasts or retrospective reports from the pages of the office copy of *The Railway World* magazine.

What was to be seen? The answer to that question (fully detailed in Chapter 3) is that by the time of my first visit there were still twenty-four sheds retaining 473 working steam locomotives. There was, if I was to catch any runs with them, little time left – their date with the cutter's torch was fast approaching! With that in mind I made three further visits north of the border during the following July and August. Into 1966, and taking into consideration it was now a race against time, I increased my incursions to seven. Although the home allocation was annihilated in May 1967, courtesy of Kingmoor TMD's foreman's predilection for dispatching his iron horses into the steam desert Scotland had become, a further twelve border crossings were undertaken.

This then is my story of those visits. This book recounts the twenty-seven months of my life during which I managed to accumulate over 4,000 steam miles in Scotland behind sixty-one different locomotives from twelve classes resourced from fifteen different sheds. The abortive journeys, long waits, the joys and euphoria when successes materialised, the disappointments when they didn't. In a never-to-be-repeated scenario, please join me on my search for steam in Scotland.

I

FOR THE LOVE OF STEAM

I AM SOMETIMES asked what prompted me to document my railway travels while on my extensive steam-chasing travels during the 1960s. My response would have been, at the time, that one day in the dim distant future I might have the time to throw it all together into a book which might interest like-minded enthusiasts hankering after the steam age railway scene encountered back then. Fast-forward half a century and during 2002–03 I had a health-imposed sabbatical period from modern-day living during which a non-railway-orientated friend asked what interests I had. My reply was my one-time all-consuming hobby of 'chasing steam'. He then suggested that it might be therapeutic to document my activities for others to read about and enjoy – perhaps bringing back memories of those days. Initially doubting his reasoning, I compiled an article detailing my visits to the West Country during 1964 and forwarded it to *Steam Days* magazine whose editor, Rex Kennedy, published it. I will forever be grateful to him because that 'success' has subsequently spawned three books (so far) and over forty articles!

Everyone should have a hobby. Rather than the more usual ones such as following a favourite football team, fishing or golf, mine was and still is the steam locomotive. Although generalised as trainspotting, upon fervent defence of my hobby I often point out that the time spent travelling to see a football team lose or lazing hours away on a riverbank without a bite or walking miles in inclement weather putting a ball down a hole are no different to my hobby. If you achieve satisfaction through it then so be it!

The steam locomotive is an awe-inspiring, living, breathing machine without which the transport of both passengers and freight through the nineteenth and the first half of the twentieth century would have been severely impaired. For sure the emissions produced by them are frowned upon by today's environmental activists but are small in comparison to the fumes from thousands of road vehicles trawling the country's motorways. The sense of anticipation of the journey ahead when a steam locomotive is being prepared to work a train is somehow missing with today's turn up and switch on scenario. The smell of steam and oil, the simmering potent power ready to be released, the crew going about their duties all add to an atmosphere that has long since disappeared. Just seconds from departure the driver, and quite often the fireman as well, could often be observed looking back along the platform for the guard's 'right away'. Doors slammed, the whistle blew and the green flag waved as the locomotive's safety valves lifted, filling the station's train shed roof and surrounding area with steam. Then to rid the locomotive of excess steam or water the injectors were operated – often thwarting any platform-end photographer's hopes of a decent departure shot. The driver opened the regulator with the first beat, shooting smoke and cinders into the air only to shut it down to avoid damage to locomotive and track upon a wheel spin on the greasy rail. Then having gained momentum to get the train on its way, and only then, can the entry in your Ian Allan *ABC* be red-lined as having been hauled by that particular locomotive – a moody, unpredictable, often aesthetically handsome beast which could, later in the journey, ride like a bucking bronco or run as sweet as a sewing machine. It would be down to the skill of the crew to tame her and get all who rely on her to their destinations. Personally, since first viewing them at Waterloo in the early 1960s, I have had an ongoing love affair with them. They have been a predominant mistress in my life for over half a century and, being the basis of this book, I defy the reader not to comprehend the reasoning as to why I spent my formative years in pursuit of them.

Not initially an enthusiast when joining BR, it wasn't until mid 1963 the disappearing steam and line closures finally fired sufficient interest to propel me out to places I had often directed prospective customers to with my job at London's Waterloo as telephone enquiry clerk. During my lunch break the 13.30 departure for Weymouth and Bournemouth West was often viewed from the end of Platform 11 and perhaps it was the sheer majesty of the 8P Merchant Navy class locomotive with its safety valves lifting and the fireman fuelling the fire in readiness for the 143-mile journey ahead that became the catalyst which sowed the seeds of a lifetime hobby. As I stood there camera, poised in readiness for the platform staff's whistle and the guard's 'right away', the power subsequently unleashed with the Pacific initially slipping (an inherent Bulleid weakness) on the greasy rail before finally finding her feet and powering the train into the distance must have sunk deep into the memory bank of an impressionable teenager. At the rear of the train ably assisting with an almighty shove was the tank engine that had brought the stock in from Clapham Yard. Within the cavernous station train shed the ear-splitting cacophony of its thunderous exhaust sent the pigeons into orbit and made any conversation nigh on impossible. It all lasted for less than a minute before the tank engine driver slammed on the brakes to bring him to a standstill alongside the ever-present gaggle of enthusiasts always resident at the country end of Platform 11. How anyone fails to be impressed with the sight and sound of a steam locomotive in full flight is *still* is beyond my comprehension.

Having initially joined British Rail(ways) 'because my parents noted my interest in local timetables' (albeit bus!), I soon realised that the majority of the, certainly clerical, workforce saw their employment not only as a means to pay the mortgage but as an extension of their hobby – enhanced perhaps by the free and reduced rate travel facilities available! One particular friend, Bill – with whom I was to subsequently travel throughout Europe – often arrived in the office on a Monday morning with tales of his travels, photographs and timetables from all over the country. 'Get out there – use your travel facilities. It's all disappearing,' he often said. He was referring to the seemingly relent less number of routes closing as a consequence of Dr Beeching's axe ('The Reshaping of British Railways' – 1963) together with increasing dieselisation ('Modernisation and Re-Equipment of the British Railways' – 1955), the consequential outcome inevitably leading to the wholesale slaughter of the steam locomotive. During the latter part of 1963 curiosity began to get the better of me and I tentatively started to venture further afield, away from the mundane commuting suburban journeys undertaken so far, to routes (in the south of England) threatened with closure. From March 1964, however, having had a birthday present from my parents of a Kodak Colorsnap 35 and now always travelling with a notebook, the addiction was taking hold of me. This camera was equipped with the latest technology! It had a lens you could change to whatever the weather was doing, i.e. bright sunshine, black-lined cloud or rain – not quite up to present-day technology but adequate enough for my needs. Over the years, having been dropped, lost and cursed at (when the film jammed), it has provided me with over 1,000 images, some of which have found their way into the railway press.

As the months counted down towards the end of steam throughout Britain, an ever-increasing number of enthusiasts could be witnessed on the scene. My interests became focused on travelling behind as many different steam locomotives as possible: rather than 'copping' a locomotive we 'haulage bashers' had to travel behind our quarry in order to red line the entry in our Ian Allan *Locoshed* books. With the scarcity of steam-hauled passenger services on offer in Scotland, this particular aspect of my hobby was, for the day visits I embarked upon, temporarily abandoned – obtaining any run with steam was difficult enough! Regrettably photography took second place, with monies being directed more at travel costs. Memories, however, remain and whenever espying a photograph in a magazine or book of a train I might have travelled on out come the notebooks and if indeed I was aboard the depicted train the relevant page gets extracted, scanned, copied and stowed away in my 'I was there' folder. It was a mad, frenetic period: the camaraderie, the sense of urgency – knowing it would all end one day. Steam was disappearing at an extraordinarily fast rate: that fact alone provided the impetus to attempt to catch every potential movement. Capitalising on this aspect, Colin Gifford's popular *Decline of Steam* book became a best seller amongst us ferroequinologists.

I sometimes wonder, if the steam locomotive's decline hadn't been so quick would such enthusiasm, such a fanatical chase, have occurred? While appreciating the run-down condition and constant failures – such frequent occurrences towards the end – I still feel privileged to have witnessed the scene and participated in the pursuit with all its attendant emotional excitement and sadness. One of my friends from that period recently contacted me in connection with a previous book and, within the communication, highlighted how lucky we were to have enjoyed the scenario, stating they were 'the best days of my life' – to which I concur. Whereas it was fun, exciting and joyful for us enthusiasts to follow steam locomotives as a hobby, for the railway employees working with such run-down machines in depots surrounded by dereliction and filth it was no joke. Their own employment was in doubt as steam sheds were closed down and I take my hat off to them for the chivalrous attitude they had towards us 'puffer nutters'.

Through all the travels contained within this volume my small attaché case (16in x 10in x 4in) went with me. All necessary requirements were contained within it – timetables, camera, Ian Allan books, notebooks, Lyons pies, Club biscuits, pens, flannel, handkerchief, stopwatch, cartons of orange drinks, sandwiches and of course a BR1 carriage key, for use in emergencies! Sturdy enough to sit on in crowded corridors of packed trains and doubling up as a pillow (albeit hard!) on overnight services, my case was in regular use through the final years of BR steam and even travelled with me throughout Europe. Having survived many domestic upheavals over the years, it now enjoys a comfortable retirement at the bottom of my 'railway' cupboard at home – containing all the documented travel information without which I could never

My case and 'equipment' – a constant companion in my years of steam chasing.

have contemplated writing a book such as this. As for apparel, the anorak was not in existence then – to the best of my knowledge it was either a raincoat or a duffle coat with its attendant toggle fasteners. Usually having commenced weekend travels directly after a day's work at the office, the obligatory tie (modern and straight edged) was always worn – albeit at peculiar angles after an overnight trip. The followers were classless. They came from all walks of life including vicars, MPs (such as Robert Adley of Winchester who has become a leading opponent to privatisation) and persons from many a varied employ-ment. I often wondered how those who did not obtain cheap travel as an employment perk could afford it all – but then again ticket checks on trains were infrequent and there were no automatic barriers back then!

Upon returning home after each escapade, or within a few days if very late back, all the necessary details collected were transferred into legibility within large A4-sized desk diaries. Separate small books kept individual locomotive

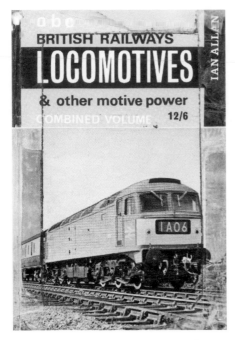

Front cover of the autumn 1964 Ian Allan   Front cover of Part 2 of an Ian Allan *ABC*.
Combined Volume.

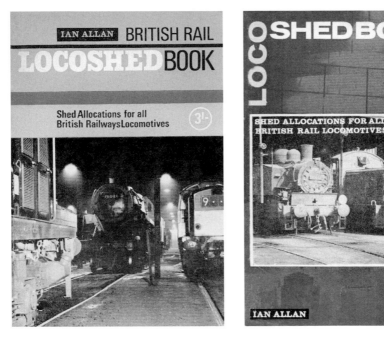

The *Locoshed* books issued by Ian Allan were essential tools in keeping up to date with the
whereabouts and numbers of steam locomotives. Here are the front covers of two issues:
autumn 1965 (left) and autumn 1966 (right).

mileages, shed visits and timed trains. I lost the pre-June 1965 notebooks from which I extracted the information but have retained all the rest. There was much to do. Each 'capture' was red-lined in my dog-eared and soot-stained Ian Allan *Locoshed* book, often amongst many entries that had been blacked out, indicating it had been withdrawn. These books were reissued quite regularly and, what with the continuous transferring (information updated courtesy of *The Railway World* magazine) of locomotives resulting from line or depot closures, much midnight oil was burnt in just attempting to keep it all current. Luckily the detailing of such minutiae came easily to me through my work as a BR train planner, where precise and accurate documentation was a necessary requirement. Then there was a surprising educational benefit in regard to the named locomotives, some of which were, to my teenage mind, unpronounce-able. References to library books or encyclopaedias were often made as to who Miles Beevor or Tennyson were, where the Solway Firth was or what Sayajirao was. It was that much more difficult back then – not having the ability to type in the search box on your smartphone! So off we go …

2

FIRST IMPRESSIONS

WITH THE TRAVELS depicted in this book commencing in 1965, perhaps it is wise to highlight a few headline-grabbing events from that year thus setting the scene. In January, arguably the most prestigious steam train ever run by BR, that conveying Sir Winston Churchill's body from London's Waterloo to Oxfordshire, received worldwide media coverage. The following month a second Beeching report was published, 'The Development of Major Trunk Routes', which recommended financial investment in just 50 per cent of the remaining 7,500 route miles. In other non-railway news that spring, Goldie, a London Zoo golden eagle, was recaptured after thirteen days of freedom, the Greater London Council (GLC) came into being and Kathy Kirby's 'I Belong' just missed out, by coming second, in the annual Eurovision Song Contest. Football wise: south of the border Manchester United won the Football League First Division title whilst Liverpool, for the first time in their history, won the FA Cup at Wembley – beating Leeds United 2-1. In Scotland Kilmarnock topped League Division One whilst Stirling Albion triumphed in Division Two.

So on Friday 28 May 1965, with recent news of Sandie Shaw having secured the top spot for a three-week run with 'Long Live Love' and Muhammad Ali having knocked out Sonny Liston with his 'Phantom Punch' in a rematch at Maine, I set forth out of the demolition site of Euston (it was being rebuilt in connection with the WCML electrification, the main casualty being the historic Doric Arch) on the 19.30 'Northern Irishman' departure for the Scottish port of Stranraer. This 406-mile 10-hour journey was my longest to date – superseding the 260-mile 6¾-hour Waterloo to Padstow made the previous July. The only section of the WCML that had been electrified by then was that between Rugby Midland and Crewe, the power either side of those locations being provided by English Electric Type 4 DLs. Although I was the sole occupant of my compartment north of Wigan, upon returning to it at Carlisle, having ascertained which locomotive had come on the front (it was Kingmoor's Black 5MT 45012), I discovered most seats were now taken.

Dawn broke much earlier in Scotland than I was used to in southern England and, although initially opting to sit in a three-a-side scenario, upon realising at Dumfries that an assisting locomotive was being attached up front, I was perfectly content to 'window hang' (a popular move by steam train aficionados!) for the remaining 2-hour journey. The assisting locomotive, sister 45467, was Dumfries (67E) allocated. The shed, which was located just a 5-minute walk to the south of the station, had an allocation of seventeen steam locomotives that May, comprising eleven Black 5s, two 76xxx, one 78xxx and three Standard 4MT tanks. The stopping services along the Port Road to Castle Douglas, together with the Kirkcudbright branch, had been withdrawn earlier that month and at the end of that year the stopping services along the former G&SWR route to Glasgow St Enoch suffered a similar fate. With the shed's workload inevitably decreasing, it lost its allocation altogether in June 1966, retaining servicing facilities until its complete closure five months later.

Dumfries, a town at which Scottish poet and lyricist Robert Burns, who left behind a magnificent legacy of poems and songs which helped define Scotland's place in the world, spent his final years, is bisected by the Nith; this river is famous for its trout and salmon, and eventually disgorges into the Solway Firth. Two other more recent residents are actor John Laurie, best known as Private 'we're all doomed' Frazer of *Dad's Army* fame, and singer-songwriter, DJ and record producer Adam Wiles (aka Calvin Harris). The town's football club, well remembered by myself from those far-off days when my father insisted on quietness when the pools results were broadcast on Saturday afternoons, is Queen of the South – founded in 1919 and just missing out on promotion out of League Division Two by coming third in the 1964–65 season.

The entire route of this 73-mile railway across the then south-west Scottish counties of Dumfries-shire, Kirkcudbrightshire and Wigtownshire was opened throughout in 1861, the objective being to offer a connection from England into a shorter sea crossing from the mainland to Belfast than the existing one via Liverpool. While indeed serving that purpose, over the intervening years, because it passed through beautiful but alas sparsely populated terrain, little local traffic was generated. Inevitably it came to the attention of Dr Beeching's accountants and, with the ability to divert the through trains via an alternative, albeit lengthier (43 miles longer) route via Mauchline and Ayr, his axe was to fall off it the following month. The politics of that decision were far from my mind that morning. The sound and sight of the two Black 5s, having passed over the River Nith, hammering away up the 1 in 73 incline to Lochanhead only confirmed, to my mind, that there can be no greater thrill in the world than being in the presence of a steam locomotive being worked hard against the gradient.

The first 20 miles of this line, part of which has now been converted to a cycle path, was double tracked. Essential window-hanging duties from the first coach became a precondition, and after having been deafened by the thunderous exhaust from both locomotives for nigh on 15 minutes upon conquering the summit at Lochanhead, the noise suddenly abated. Now, the opportunity to look back was taken, and the mesmerising sight of this lengthy train snaking its way through the early morning sunshine-swathed countryside was beheld.

All too soon, at the former junction station of the recently deceased 10-mile-long Kirkcudbright branch of Castle Douglas, the assisting locomotive was detached. This left 45012 to struggle on alone with her heavy train, which included at least two sleeping cars, up the 1 in 80 incline to the remote Loch Skerrow signal box before easing over the impressive Little and Big Fleet viaducts prior to making one final assault up the 1 in 76 incline to the line's

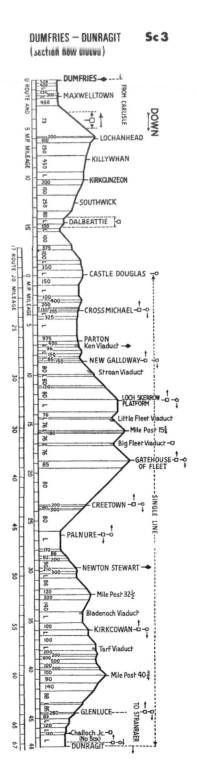

The gradient profile of the Dumfries to Dunragit section of the Port Road, a line that closed in June 1965.

summit at Gatehouse of Fleet. Although not booked to call at the intermediate stations west of Castle Douglas as they were crossing places on the now single-tracked line, we had to slow for token exchange with the signalman. Speed was therefore never great and after each slowing 45012 was once again opened up, sending nearby grazing sheep running.

We could all relax then with a 7-mile descent to the River Cree levels of Palnure and Newton Stewart, followed by a series of lesser gradients, prior to arriving into Stranraer just 15 minutes late at 05.30. Even after half a century I can still recall that early morning sun-drenched dawn ride. There were glimpses of the Solway Firth's shimmering waters on one side with sheep-adorned Galloway Hills on the other, all the while passing through stations furnished with totem signs of a colour scheme I had not previously witnessed: the distinctive Scottish sky-blue background with white lettering. What an initiation to, for me, a new country.

So now with 2 hours to wait, I contemplated walking the streets in order to visit Stranraer (67F) shed, having failed to pack my *British Locomotive Shed Directory* (an Ian Allan publication often referred to in order to locate steam sheds or cross cities), but decided against getting lost and missing the solitary morning departure at 07.25 for Ayr.

'The Northern Irishman', having completed its 406-mile 10-hour journey from London, is seen at Stranraer Harbour on the morning of Saturday 29 May 1965. Carlisle Kingmoor's 30-year-old Black 5 45012 rests after her 107-mile journey over the undulating gradients of the Port Road. The Stanier 5MT was subsequently transferred to Barrow, being withdrawn in October 1966.

The only egress out of Stranraer by either road or rail, involved some serious hill climbing. Ayr-bound trains had to ascend nearly 14 miles of incline, including a 3-mile section as steep as 1 in 57, to the Chirmorie moorland plateau, after which, at MP 16½, an 8-mile descent led to further climbing through Pinmore to MP 4 before finally surmounting a series of humps prior to arriving at Ayr. Completed in piecemeal sections by several different companies, this route through Rabbie Burns' 'kingdom' – he having been born at Alloway, a one-time intermediate station on the Heads of Ayr branch (closed 1968) – was finally opened throughout in 1877, ultimately being taken over by the G&SWR. Having thwarted Beeching's attempt at closure in the 1960s, the line remains open today – although its future once again appears in doubt with the move of Stena Line to the new, non-rail-connected port of Cairnryan in November 2011.

After a 1¾-hour fume-filled DMU journey, I arrived into Ayr at just gone 09.00. It was here in 1315 that the first ever Scottish Parliament was held with locally born (at the nearby Turnberry Castle) Robert the Bruce – arguably Scotland's most popular king who reigned from 1306 to 1329. A one-time centre of textile industries, Ayr, with its fine sandy beaches, is perhaps better recognised nowadays as a holiday resort. Located just 2 miles south of Prestwick airport, the town's football club, Ayr United – founded in 1910 – is yet another Saturday afternoon name well remembered. Ayr's (67C) steam shed was actually located almost a mile north of Ayr itself – at Newton-on-Ayr. The shed had Scotland's largest remaining allocation of Hughes Crabs 2-6-0s (17) for use throughout the Ayrshire coalfield together with ten Black 5s and three 76xxx for passenger traffic. Closure to steam came in the October of the following year after the transfer in of suitable DLs for the remaining coal services.

I had purchased (by post) a *Scottish Railfans* publication at 1s allegedly specifying all the remaining steam-worked passenger services throughout Scotland. As always with those somewhat speculative publications, the ever-changing motive-power scene usually renderers it out of date as soon as the print dries. So it was in this case: the 09.20 (SO 14 June to 21 August) Heads of Ayr (a station specifically catering for the masses visiting the nearby Butlin's Holiday Camp) to Edinburgh Princes Street, shown as an Ayr Black 5, hove into view formed of a DMU! It was all part of the 'excitement' in regard to the hit-and-miss scenario encountered during those days, the inability to keep abreast of the ever-changing steam scene being often experienced. The disappointments were quickly forgotten when successes in the form of services not purportedly steam worked turning up unexpectedly. In this particular instance, with

This is the front cover of the *Scottish Railfans* book that detailed which passenger trains were booked for steam power. In a constantly changing scenario, this was not always the case!

no other depicted steam services in the locality, an 82-mile 2½-hour journey was accordingly endured.

This lengthy journey, which would have been so much more enjoyable had it been steam hauled, took me through mile after mile of uncharted territory. Only having brought with me a Scottish timetable and no map or atlas, it was more akin to a mystery tour, with lines peeling off at the myriad junctions en route to God knows where! Opened throughout in 1840, at first the line hugged the coast through Troon and Irvine before turning north-east then passing through Dalry where the Scottish people once rebelled against episcopacy. The scenic Barr and Castle Semple Lochs were then viewed before the Renfrewshire conurbations of Johnstone and Paisley hoved into sight.

After departure from Paisley Gilmour Street, we took the freight-only spur through the West Street Tunnel continuing past Polmadie (66A) over the River Clyde and on to former Caledonian Railway metals, opened in 1869 through the counties of Lanarkshire and West Lothian. Bradshaw opined when travelling over the line: 'a district of country rich in mineral wealth, beautiful scenery

celebrated far and wide as the orchard of Scotland famous for its fine fruit'
After calling at Holytown (née Carfin), Shotts and Addiewell, an eventual
arrival time of 12.07 was achieved into Edinburgh's Princes Street station. Just
prior to arriving there another steam shed, Dalry Road (64C), could be espied
from the train. Compared with its North British rival, the nearby Haymarket
shed, this Caledonian shed was a somewhat paltry affair. Its allocation that May
had dwindled to a mere ten LMS Black 5s and five LNER B1s – its demise
concurrent with Princes Street station closure.

The Caledonian Railway opened the Princes Street station I visited that
day in 1870, itself replacing an earlier 1848 terminal at Lothian Street. Rebuilt,
following a major fire, in the 1890s, the station was provided with seven platforms and an 850ft-long bayed roof, and it for sure portrayed the opulence of
the period. After nationalisation of the railways, it was always going to be the
intent to concentrate rail services within cities at the fewest termini feasible
and, with Waverley station a short distance along Princes Street itself, by the
1960s, Princes Street station, taking into account the ever-decreasing local
services, was deemed superfluous. What had decimated the local passenger
train usage was, as ever with commuter travel, the more frequent bus services.
I was personally unaware of its impending demise at the time of my journey,
but upon the remaining main-line services to Glasgow Central, Stirling and
English cities being diverted to Waverley, the station was closed just over three
months later. The site was levelled in 1969–70 with the West Approach Road
being built along the former track bed. More recently, in May 2014, the much-
delayed Edinburgh tram system commenced running and, although operating
over a far shortened distance from the original proposal, had the Princes Street
terminus survived the years the trams would certainly would have hammered
the final nail into its coffin.

Another disappointment was to follow. The 13.20 departure for Carstairs –
another train depicted as being a steam-worked service in my *Scottish Railfans*
book – was worked by Type 1 Clayton D8587. One hundred and seventeen
of these centre-cabbed Bo-Bo (Class 17) diesel locomotives had been built,
commencing in 1962, but due to reliability problems were deemed the least
successful DL design ever – all being withdrawn by 1971. A steam chaser always
lives in hope and finally, after 10 steamless hours, deliverance came with the
arrival into Carstairs of Kingmoor's Britannia 70005 *John Milton* working the
09.25 Crewe–Perth train.

This was my first Brit – little did I know then that over the next three years
I was to accumulate over 8,000 miles with thirty-eight of her sisters. The hour
I was to spend on this train took me further north than I had ever been before

Saturday 29 May 1965, and while waiting at Carstairs for the 09.25 Crewe–Perth train and unaware that it was to be my first run with a member of the Britannia class, an unidentified sister, having been shorn of her number and nameplates heads, a northbound parcels service.

Crossing over the junction with the Edinburgh branch at Carstairs, Crewe-built Black 5 44726 takes the WCML route back to her home depot of Kingmoor with another parcels service.

and was to pass by three more steam sheds on the 46¾-mile journey to Stirling – Carstairs (66E) depot, accessible via a footbridge off the Glasgow end of the platform, being the first. This former CR shed, which was to close in December 1966, had, at the time, a home allocation of five Fairburn tanks and eleven Black 5s. The complexity of lines this train travelled through was bewildering. A mere 16 miles further north, having passed through the hometown of snooker legend John Higgins (colloquially known as the Wizard of Wishaw), another ex CR shed, Motherwell (66B), could be viewed. A slightly larger allocation of twenty locomotives dwelled here, the majority (fourteen) being the inevitable Black 5s, and the balance being BR Standards. This shed became one of the final seven, lasting until spring 1967. We then passed Mossend Yard – already large back, then it is planned to become Scotland's International Railfreight Park. With both Coatbridge and Larbert being called at en route just prior to arriving into my destination of Stirling, the shed there (65J) could be viewed from the train. I was never a 'spotter' and therefore no notes were made at the time as to its occupants – subsequent research revealed that ten Black 5s were housed there.

Stirling, the one-time capital of Scotland and ancient seat of Scottish kings just a few miles from where the Battle of Bannockburn (1314) happened, is a historic garrison town and was bestowed a city status in 2002 as part of Queen Elizabeth II's Golden Jubilee celebrations. A further celebratory fact the year of my journey was, having topped Division Two that month, Stirling Albion Football Club was promoted for the 1965–66 season. The station, opened by the Scottish Central Railway in 1848, was extensively rebuilt by the Caledonian Railway in 1915 and was one of the more pleasant stations to spend time at as it was adorned with flowers and fresh paint at the time of my visit.

Although the prime motivation for this 'day' trip had been triggered by the impending closure of the Dumfries–Stranraer route, as always trying to pack in as much as possible, I had deliberately engineered the itinerary to arrive here at Stirling in the hope of catching a run with one of the famed Gresley 'streaks'. Was my guide going to let me down again? The 13.30 'Grampian' Aberdeen–Glasgow, with a Stirling departure time of 16.45, was shown to be an Aberdeen (Ferryhill) LNER 4-6-2 A4 and, upon seeing 60034 *Lord Faringdon* arrive bang on time just 30 minutes later, I let out a sigh of relief.

This was another first: I had only seen photographs of these outstandingly handsome, sleek, aerodynamic machines in publications such as *The Railway World* magazine and to be in the presence of a real-life example was undeniably awesome. Although still working a few services out of King's Cross as late as 1963, its demise in England was impending, but at the time I was too naive as to be aware of it, and being up close to one of these 'streaks' with their

My first catch of one of Gresley's famous 'streaks': LNER A4 60034 *Lord Faringdon* arrives into Stirling with the 13.30 'Grampian' Aberdeen–Glasgow Buchanan Street. For the first ten years of her life, while allocated to various ECML depots, she carried the name *Peregrine*, immigrating to Scotland in October 1963.

mournful, haunting chime whistle was wonderfully exhilarating to a teenager in love with steam. On this train, as on many other A4 runs caught later in my travels, the crew seemed to lap up the attention of all and sundry, and their enthusiasm shone through as they made it a personal challenge to maintain the tight schedule. As if seeing one wasn't enough, upon arrival into Glasgow's Buchanan Street station at 17.30 the simultaneously timed departure of 'The St Mungo' with sister 60019 *Bittern* was also witnessed. I knew it would have been highly unlikely to have made the same minute cross-platform connection but, just 5 minutes later, a more than adequate compensatory Standard Caprotti, 73151, powered me back up through the 430-yard-long tunnel immediately outside the station with the 17.35 Dunblane departure. Together with her ten consecutively numbered sisters, this locomotive's home depot of St Rollox (65B) was passed en route about 2 miles out of Buchanan Street, of which 73151 herself was a lifelong (nine years four months) resident. Whilst the A4's exhaust was, in my opinion, a somewhat feminine affair, the Caprotti was the exact opposite. I was unaware at the time of St Rollox's drivers' predilection for driving locomotives hard (i.e. regulator in the roof), and starting away from both the Cumbernauld and Greenhill station stops, a fine display of cinders and black smoke was dispatched high into the evening air; her barking exhaust was surely heard for miles around. All too soon my alighting station of Larbert

Compared with the quietly efficient exhaust of the A4s, the Standard 5MTs, working services over the former Caledonian main line out of Glasgow, were ear-splitting. Seen here storming away from Larbert with the 17.35 Glasgow Buchanan Street–Dunblane is lifelong St Rollox resident 73151. Ten of these Caprotti-equipped Standards were allocated to 65B, being gradually withdrawn as more DLs became available; this example lasted until August 1966.

was upon me and, reluctantly adhering to my pre-planned itinerary to head for the night train south from Edinburgh, I watched in awe as the Standard 5MT accelerated away northwards.

My next train, the 18.30 Stirling–Edinburgh Waverley, was another dis-appointment – allegedly being steam operated but turning up with D6119. Yet another short-lived diesel locomotive type, these North British Type 2s (Class 21), delivered from 1958 onwards, ceased to exist a mere ten years later, having suffered reliability problems. This train, via Falkirk Grahamston, took me past Grangemouth Junction, from where a branch to Grangemouth Docks diverged. Onwards to Edinburgh and, having sped through the then open sta-tion of Manuel (current terminus of the Bo'ness & Kinneil preserved railway) and after passing Haymarket TMD (formerly 64B and one-time home of the famed ECML Pacifics), arrival into the impressive Edinburgh Waverley sta-tion at 19.30 allowed sufficient time to obtain a much-desired cup of soup. St Margarets-allocated Standard 2-6-4 80114, on station pilot duties, was the only steam noting during my time there that evening.

Edinburgh, the capital city of Scotland, is often referred to as the 'Athens of the North' – a nod to the large number of historic, prestigious buildings and museums – not forgetting its castle and the beautifully laid out Princes Street gardens. The city was also witness to the signing of the 1707 Act of Union, not, as is often falsely rumoured, in a cellar now part of an Italian restaurant, but at the old Scottish parliament building on Parliament Square. A host of famous people were born in the city, such as former Labour Prime Minister Tony Blair, track cyclist and Olympic Games gold and silver medal winner Sir Chris Hoy and actor and film producer Sean Connery, to name but a few.

Edinburgh Waverley station is situated in a steep, narrow valley between the medieval Old Town and the eighteenth-century New Town. The valley was formerly occupied by Nor Loch – a sheet of stagnant water subsequently drained to allow the North Bridge to cross the valley. The present three-iron-span and steel structure supported by huge sandstone piers, which passes high above the station's central section, dates from 1897. Waverley Bridge lies to the west side of the station, which, by means of ramps, affords vehicular access and provides two of the six pedestrian entrances to the station.

With the explosion of railway travel throughout Britain, three railway companies built stations in the valley in the course of the 1840s. The collective name 'Waverley', after the same-titled novels by Sir Walter Scott, was used for all three upon the through route to Carlisle being opened. In 1868 the North British Railway acquired the stations of its rivals, demolished all three, and built the station, which I was at during this journey. From its opening in its current form by the eastward tunnelled extension from Haymarket, Waverley has always been the principal railway station in Edinburgh. Some years after the ECML electrified services commenced (1991), further sections of the station were extensively refurbished, incorporating two new through platforms and the electrification of platforms 12 to 18 in connection with the electric trains for the reopened (2010) Airdrie–Bathgate rail link. More recently the glazed roof of Waverley station was entirely replaced with new strengthened clear glass panels, greatly increasing the amount of natural light in the station. Plans have recently (2015) been proposed to extend three further platforms in an attempt to cope with an expected doubling of passenger usage – the electrification of the Glasgow line via Falkirk being a major factor – over the next ten years.

My train home that night, the 20.20 Edinburgh Waverley–King's Cross, had Type 5 Deltic (Class 55) D9003 *St Paddy* at the helm. She was a representative of twenty-two constructed during 1961–62 to replace fifty-five Gresley Pacifics on the ECML express services. Holding sway for two decades, they themselves have succumbed to progress, all being withdrawn by 1981–82, with six surviving into preservation. Light was fading as I passed through the final steam shed sighting of my trip. Unusually straddling the main running line, St

Margarets (64A), located 1¾ miles into the journey, had over forty locomotives still allocated there including LNER examples of A4s (two), A3s (two), V2s (eight) and B1s (fifteen). Had I ever been a 'spotter', this being the tenth shed I had passed near or viewed during that trip, my notebook would have been overflowing! A punctual arrival into King's Cross at 05.59 on the Sunday morning (having been diverted via Lincoln due to engineering works) thus completed my 1,105-mile outing that May weekend. There was always going to be highs and lows associated with steam chasing back in the 1960s. However, the obvious disappointment in three of the scheduled steam services being diesel was compensated by the wonderful scenic entry into Scotland aboard 'The Northern Irishman' coupled with catching a run with an iconic A4 on 'The Grampian'. Funds precluded a quick return to Scotland, but, with steam locomotives from classes I had yet to have runs with unique to services north of the border, it would only be a matter of time!

3

THE MAIN PLAYERS

SO HAVING DETAILED my first journey over the border perhaps now is the time to set the scene insofar as to which classes of steam locomotives remained by May 1965. Excluding the 'visitors' from England, which I will summarise at the end of this chapter, there were just 473 surviving locomotives from eighteen different classes residing at twenty-four motive-power depots.

LMS Fairburn Tanks

Designed by Fairburn, 277 of these 4MT 2-6-4 tanks were constructed between 1945 and 1951 at Brighton (41) and Derby (236) works. Based on his predecessor Stanier's 2-6-4Ts, they were allocated throughout Britain (excepting the WR) used mainly on suburban passenger services. By May 1965 just twenty-six remained on Scottish soil, the two sheds of Polmadie and Greenock retaining the majority for the suburban services not being operated by either DMU or DL out of Glasgow Central. Just one, 42274, survived into 1967, while two others made it into preservation.

LMS Crabs

Designed by Hughes, 245 of these 5MT 2-6-0s were constructed at Horwich (70) and Crewe (175) between 1926 and 1932. The, at the time, unusually high running plate earned them the nickname 'Crabs' – a reference to the resemblance to a crab's pincers of the outside cylinders and valve motion. Another suggestion is that the nickname refers to the 'scuttling' motion felt on the footplate when the locomotive is being worked hard due largely to the inclined cylinders producing a sensation that it is akin to walking along

The only photograph I have of an active 'Crab' is here at Goole in October 1966 –
Birkenhead's 42942 powering a returning Liverpool-bound rail tour.

the track. Allocated throughout the LMR, NER and ScR, just twenty-one
remained on Scottish territory, of which seventeen were allocated to Ayr for
the Ayrshire coalfield traffic. The only occasion I 'copped' them in Scotland
was in September 1966 (there being only six extant by then) while passing Ayr
shed – a lengthy line of withdrawn examples stored in the open awaiting their
inevitable fate. Three have survived into preservation.

LMS Black 5s

In the history of British steam locomotive none have ever been as univer-
sally popular as Stanier's 5MT 4-6-0 Black 5s. They were undoubtedly the
most proficient design of general-purpose mixed-traffic engine ever seen in
Britain, subsequently proving suitable for almost any duty. Construction commenced in 1934 and finished in 1951 (suspended 1939–42), when numbers
eventually totalled 842, being distributed the length and breadth of the former
LMS system. Only four examples were named and nationally, by the end of
1965, numbers were down to 627, the ScR's quota being approximately ninety.
Widely distributed amongst all twenty-four remaining Scottish sheds, except
the 62 group, the largest contingent was at Perth (twenty-five), which once
peaked at seventy-five in 1950. Although catching many on Scottish soil, in
particular on services emanating out of Carlisle, only a meagre nine were

home-based examples – coincidentally the same number made it to the final May. Eventually accumulating runs with a third of the class (281) by the end of BR steam in August 1968, a further eight of the eighteen that survived into preservation have subsequently been bagged.

LMS Moguls

One hundred and twenty-eight of these Ivatt-designed 2MT 2-6-0s were constructed between 1946 and 1953, split between Crewe, Darlington and Swindon. Allocated to all regions excepting the SR, they were ideal for working (both passenger and freight) over lightly laid branch lines. The eleven that remained in Scotland were thinly spread between six depots. My only noting of one was at Arbroath one summer Saturday morning when an immaculately turned out 46464, Dundee's only remaining example, was shunting freight wagons – a photograph of which is on p. 69. December 1966 saw the final survivor, 46451, withdrawn. Seven survived into preservation, including the aforementioned numerically palindromic numbered 46464.

LNER A4s

What can be said that already hasn't about these iconic machines? Thirty-five of these streamlined Gresley-designed 8P 4-6-2s were constructed at Doncaster between 1935 and 1938. Put to work on the fastest of expresses over the ECML between King's Cross and Scotland, one of them, 60022 *Mallard*, still holds the world's fastest speed for a steam locomotive of 126mph achieved in 1938. To work the non-stop London–Scotland expresses many examples were equipped with corridor tenders enabling the crews to changeover while on the move. After having been suspended since the Second World War, the ScR authorities had reintroduced the 3-hour expresses between Aberdeen and Glasgow in the early 1960s using North British Type 2 DLs, but their disastrous reliability forced the authorities to look elsewhere for alternative power. In February 1962 A4 60027 *Merlin* was successfully tested, which led to a remarkable, and perhaps unique, replacement of diesel power with steam. To augment the existing allocation of seven A4s nine further examples, ousted from their ECML duties by the Deltics, migrated from English sheds. It shouldn't be forgotten that while awaiting the arrival of the English A4s two A3s 60090 *Grand Parade* and 60094 *Colorado*, both St Rollox allocated, stepped in to cover the shortfall. Ten A4s were still on Scottish soil as of May 1965 and, always prioritising their workings whenever in Scotland, I was fortunate to collect runs with five of them. Allocated to Ferryhill (seven), St Margarets (two) and St Rollox (one), with the exception of 60024 *Kingfisher*, which was transferred from 64A to 61B in early

1966, all remained at their depots until withdrawal. The final two, 60019 *Bittern* and 60024 *Kingfisher* were withdrawn in September 1966. Six have made it into preservation, although two, 60008 *Dwight D. Eisenhower* and 60010 *Dominion of Canada*, were exported and 60022 *Mallard* is on static display at the NRM York. All took part in The Great Gathering held at the NRM locations of York and Shildon during 2013–14, the overseas examples being temporarily repatriated. The three active members – 60007 *Sir Nigel Gresley*, 60009 *Union of South Africa* and 60019 *Bittern* – are alive and well, and work a great many trains throughout the UK on both main and preserved lines.

The expresses, four of which were 3-hour, they worked were:

	A	B	C	D
Glasgow	08.25	10.00	14.05	17.30
Aberdeen	11.25	13.41	17.40	20.30

	C	D	A	B
Aberdeen	07.10	09.30	13.30	17.15
Glasgow	10.10	13.30	17.30	20.15

(A) 'The Grampian'   (C) 'The Bon Accord'
(B) 'The Granite City'   (D) 'The St Mungo'

LNER A3s

Seventy-nine of these Gresley-designed 7P 4-6-2 locomotives were constructed between 1922 and 1935 at Doncaster (fifty-nine) and North British (twenty). They had worked over the ECML, Waverley and GCR routes for many years but by May 1965 just three Scottish allocated examples remained – all at St Margarets. They were 60100 *Spearmint* (until June 1965), 60041 *Salmon Trout* (until December 1965) and 60052 *Prince Palatine* (until January 1966). Forever regretting 'letting go' the opportunity to catch one in normal service (60112 *St Simon* at Newcastle in August 1964), it wasn't until May 1968 that the matter was rectified: by catching Alan Pegler's preserved 60103 (4472) *Flying Scotsman* out of St Pancras.

LNER A2s

This class of locomotive was a somewhat mixed bag. The first twenty-five of these 7MT 4-6-2s were designed by Thompson and were constructed or rebuilt at Doncaster (twenty-one) and Darlington (four) between 1943 and 1947. The remaining fifteen were designed by Peppercorn and were all constructed at

There were but three Gresley A3s remaining in Scotland by the time I first visited – none of which I saw. Here at Newcastle, in August 1964, New England-allocated 41-year-old 60112 *St Simon* prepares to work the 01.00 ex King's Cross forward to Edinburgh Waverley.

Doncaster during 1947–48. Similar to other classes working ECML services, they were ousted by dieselisation during the early 1960s. The six remaining within Scotland were at Polmadie (three) and Dundee (three). Polmadie's allocation were substitutions for the recently withdrawn Stanier Pacifics and, being disliked by the former LMS drivers which highlighted their 'alleged inferiority', were withdrawn by the summer of 1965; it was left to the Dundee examples, kept in excellent nick, to fly the flag over the following year. Always liable to work the summer Saturday ECML services north of Edinburgh, they were often used to replace the ailing A4s on the 3-hour expresses out of Aberdeen during 1966. The first to be withdrawn, fortunately not until after I caught a run with her, was 60528 *Tudor Minstrel* in June 1966 – a photograph of which is on p. 74. Then sister 60530 *Sayajirao* succumbed that November, followed a month later by the now preserved 60532 *Blue Peter*.

LNER V2s

One hundred and eighty-four of these Gresley-designed 6MT 2-6-2 locomotives were constructed at Doncaster (25) and Darlington (159) between 1936 and 1944. They were the most successful of the LNER's mixed-traffic designs and worked both passenger and freight throughout the ECML from King's

A visitor to the Bluebell Railway, Sussex, in October 2003, was the preserved V2 2-6-2 60800 *Green Arrow*, she having been withdrawn at King's Cross in August 1962. (Gerald Butler)

Cross to Aberdeen. These engines were often lauded as the locomotives that won the war, during which they were frequently called upon to haul loads far in excess of their design capabilities. Only eight were named and, with numbers being decimated by dieselisation from 1962 onwards, a mere thirteen remained on ScR's books – St Margarets (eight) and Dundee (five) by May 1965. Working the summer Saturday dated services or standing in for DL failures, from a personal point of view, having spent many hours heading for trains they 'might' have worked, I found them particularly elusive. Finally catching up with one in August 1966, they were all gone within months, the last withdrawal being 60836. Only 60800 *Green Arrow* has survived into preservation and is at the NRM York.

LNER B1s

Introduced in 1942, but constructed over a lengthy ten-year period due to wartime conditions, these Thompson-designed 5MT 4-6-0 B1s, eventually totalling 410, were allocated to the ER (260), NER (80) and ScR (70). The first forty constructed were named after various species of antelope, thus bestowing their epithet of 'Bongos'. As the numbers increased it became impossible to find enough antelope species to continue this policy, and with the exception of a handful designated after directors of the LNER, most of them remained anonymous. Withdrawals, however, began in 1961, accelerated by BR's dieselisation policies of ER and NER passenger services. The ECML depots of St Margarets (fifteen) and Thornton Junction (eleven) retained the majority of the forty-five remaining in Scotland. Used predominantly on freight, it was only with short-dated summer Saturday passenger services that there was any hope of haulage with them – my own catches amount to a derisory three. Both 61072 and 61180 survived until the Scottish cull of May 1967, with two other English sisters making it into preservation.

LNER J37s
One hundred and four of these Reid-designed 0-6-0 5F locomotives were constructed between 1914 and 1921 at North British (sixty-nine) and Cowlairs (thirty-five). Although some went to Carlisle and Berwick, the majority were allocated throughout the former LNER system within Scotland. Of the twenty-four remaining the lion's share were at Thornton Junction (nine) and Dundee (eight), just three (64602, 11 and 20) making it until the end of 1966.

A very clean 0-6-0 J36 65288 is seen at Dunfermline on Sunday 16 October 1966. She had been spruced up to participate in a Fife lines brake van rail tour six days later. (Keith Lawrence)

LNER J36s

One hundred and sixty-eight of these 0-6-0 Holmes-designed 2F locomotives, produced between 1888 and 1900, were constructed at three works within Scotland – the majority at Cowlairs. Twenty-five of them were sent to France during the First World War, and all acquired names associated with battles, generals or soldiers in recognition of their service. Not being a spotter, I'm uncertain if I ever witnessed one – only nine remained by May 1965. Spread thinly between five depots, two (65288 and 65345) outlasted all other ScR steam, being withdrawn in June 1967. An earlier withdrawal, 65243 *Maude*, is at the NRM York.

LNER J38s

Thirty-five of these 0-6-0 Gresley-designed 6F locomotives, all produced in 1926, were constructed at Darlington. They spent their entire lives working the heavy coal trains on the former NBR lines in the Fife and Lothian coalfields, together with freight to Leith and other docks. Of the twenty-three remaining, twelve were at Thornton Junction and eleven at Dunfermline. The last withdrawals in April 1967 were 65901 and 65929.

BR Standard 5MT

One hundred and seventy-two of these versatile Riddles-designed 4-6-0 5MT locomotives were constructed at Derby (130) and Doncaster (42) between 1951 and 1957. With the exception of twenty examples allocated to the SR, named after Arthurian legends, these Standards follow on from Stanier's Black 5MTs and were initially allocated throughout the former LMS routes; subsequent reallocations, however, saw them spread nationwide. Thirty locomotives (73125–54) were equipped with Caprotti valve gear, as an experiment to enhance the economics of coal consumption. May 1965 saw forty-five still extant in Scotland – the three Glasgow sheds of Corkerhill (fourteen), Polmadie (eleven) and St Rollox (ten) retaining the largest allocations. All the St Rollox locomotives were of the Caprotti variation and put out some fine performances on the Buchanan Street services. The last withdrawals were 73059, 60, 4, 79 and 146. Five others have survived into preservation.

BR Standard 4MT

One hundred and fifteen of these Riddles-designed 4MT 2-6-0 locomotives were constructed between 1952 and 1957 at Doncaster (seventy) and Horwich (forty-five). They were allocated to all regions, except the WR, for use on cross-country and freight work – the latter particularly useful in view

The only Scottish representative of the BR Standard 4MT 2-6-0s that I had a run with was Beattock's 76098 at the rear of an Anglo-Scottish train in August 1966. One of the four that survived into preservation, 76084 is seen departing Sheringham while participating in the North Norfolk Railways 2013 Autumn Gala.

of weight-restricted sidings often used. Thirty-seven were still on Scottish soil in May 1965 spread between ten depots, none of which housed double figures. The last withdrawals were 76000, 46, 94, 8 and 104, with four others surviving into preservation.

BR Standard 3MT

A mere twenty of these Riddles-designed 3MT 2-6-0 class, built as a tender version of the 82xxx 3MT, were constructed at Swindon during 1954. Shared between the NER and ScR, the class was distinctive in having a high running plate, making the 5ft 3in driving wheels appear disproportionately small. This was the last class of steam locomotive on BR to remain complete before suffering its first withdrawal. Of the ten remaining in Scotland, Hurlford had six, the final five (77005, 7, 17, 8 and 9) being withdrawn in the autumn of 1966.

BR Standard 2MT

Sixty-five of these Riddles-designed 2MT 2-6-0s, the smallest of the BR standards, were constructed at Darlington between 1952 and 1956. Ideal for lightweight passenger services, the need for them within Scotland by 1965 had all but ceased, the services they had worked having been withdrawn or

A class I never witnessed in Scotland were any of the BR Standard 2MT 78xxx. Crewe South-allocated 78010 is seen in ex works condition at Derby in August 1964.

Twenty-three-year-old Vulcan Foundry-built WD 2-8-0 90560 at rest on Sunday 16 October 1966 at Alloa shed. She became one of the final seven withdrawn the following spring. (Keith Lawrence)

dieselised. Just ten remained in Scotland, with Bathgate (six) having the largest allocation; the last withdrawal was 78051.

BR Standard 4MTT

One hundred and fifty-five of these Riddles-designed 4MT 2-6-4Ts were constructed at Brighton (130), Derby (15) and Doncaster (10) between 1951 and 1956. These popular performers were built specifically for suburban passenger traffic and were based on its Stanier and Fairburn predecessors. Allocated to all regions, bar the WR, forty-seven remained active throughout Scotland, the largest groups being at the Glasgow sheds of Polmadie (thirteen), Corkerhill (eleven) and St Margarets (eight). The last withdrawals were 80004, 45, 6, 86, 116 and 20. Fifteen survived into preservation, including 80002, which performed train-heating duties at Cowlairs for a number of months after the May 1967 cull of ScR steam.

BR WD 8Fs

Seven hundred and thirty-three of these Riddles-designed 8F 2-8-0 locomotives were bought, by the LNER and BR, from the War Department; they had been constructed at either the North British or Vulcan works between 1943 and 1946. Allocated throughout all regions, many saw service overseas during the Second World War. Twenty-four remained on Scottish soil at sheds within the Fife and Lothian coalfields. The last withdrawals were 90071, 386, 468, 89, 560 and 96.

No story of steam in Scotland would be complete without the sizable contribution made by English-based 'marauding' representatives. Gateshead Pacifics and V2s came down the ECML, and Holbeck's Jubilees came over Ais Gill to both WCML and G&SWR metals. But without doubt the largest number of interlopers were residents at Carlisle's Kingmoor shed, once coded 68A as part of the Scottish system. This shed's foreman's propensity for dispatching his Black 5s, Britannias, Clans and 9Fs over the border into Scotland was nectar to the steam enthusiast, his steeds often penetrating as far north as Aberdeen. After Scotland rid itself of its home allocation, still they were sent over the border; only the demise of 12A, at the end of 1967, stopped the practice!

4

THE FIFE COAST VISIT

DURING THE EARLY days of my railway enthusiasm I tended to concentrate on line closures – not all of which had steam-operated services. Always wiser after the event, this resulted in losing out on travels with many classes of steam locomotives that, in the meantime, became extinct. Oh well – I couldn't be everywhere at once and I had to prioritise my outings as I saw fit. To this end the objective of my second weekend trip to Scotland, in July 1965, was primarily to travel over the 'doomed' Fife Coast route between Thornton and Leuchars Junctions via Crail and St Andrews.

Earlier that month the Australians had monopolised the Lawn Tennis Championship at Wimbledon, with Roy Emerson and Margaret Smith winning the singles. Then a few days later Great Train Robber Ronnie Biggs escaped from Wandsworth Prison. Other newsworthy events from that month were Sir Alec Douglas-Home's sudden resignation as leader of the Conservative Party (succeeded by Edward Heath) following the Labour victory the previous year and the boxer Freddie Mills committing suicide. Musically, The Rolling Stones' '(I Can't Get No) Satisfaction' held the top spot all that month.

It was Friday 23 July 1965 and I once again selected the 19.30 'Northern Irishman' as the starting point of this trip, noting at the Euston buffer stops two of Willesden's Standard 2MTs, 78018 and 78060, having brought in ECS for the overnight services. After departing a mere 6 minutes late, the train then lost nearly an hour between Crewe and Carlisle – I either didn't note or know the reasons. Even at that early stage of my railway travels the desire to take runs behind as many different steam locomotives as possible, which was to morph into being categorised as a 'haulage basher', was beginning to

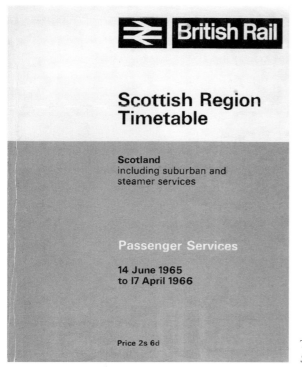

The front cover of the 1965
Scottish Region Timetable.

manifest within me. Why am I saying that? My original plan to alight from 'The Northern Irishman' at Carlisle to catch the 03.21 Ayr departure were abruptly changed upon seeing a required Britannia, 70002 *Geoffrey Chaucer*, backing down to take the train on to Stranraer. After quickly double checking with the ever-present appropriate timetable (to ascertain that both trains called at Dumfries), I reboarded the London train for 32¾ miles of Brit haulage, observing St Margarets-allocated A4 60027 *Merlin*, perhaps having come off a Waverley-routed service, simmering away on the up side of the station.

Dawn was now breaking and having passed through Gretna Green, the renowned location for underage English couples' elopement to marry legally, I alighted from 'The Northern Irishman' at Dumfries at 03.47. This route from Carlisle to Glasgow was opened throughout in 1850, with passengers initially having to change trains at Gretna prior to the G&SWR (née Glasgow, Dumfries & Carlisle Railway), negotiating running rights with the CR south thereof. At 125 miles it was lengthier than the Caledonian route via Beattock but was reduced to 116 miles when the Barrhead cut-off was opened in 1873. It really came into prominence three years later, after the Midland Railway, having forged its main line over the Pennines, then ran over these G&SWR metals in order to access Glasgow.

After having witnessed the Steamer bound train's departure on its new route, the 1870-built and closed to local passenger traffic in 1943 cut-off via Mauchline, Annbank and Ayr (the Port Road having closed the previous month), I fully expected the 04.14 Ayr train to be unaffected by the London trains late running, but that was not the case. The even later running train eventually turned up at 05.21 (67 minutes late)! Now thoroughly awake, I was about to enjoy a journey that 'daytime only' enthusiasts would miss out on. Just the four of us – the driver, fireman, guard and the sole passenger (me) – with Kingmoor's Black 5MT 45259 1 BSK and three vans, set off on a 73-minute 58-mile journey over the former G&SWR metals through the beautiful countryside of southern Scotland. Frequently intertwining with the adjacent A76 and the River Nith, the competent locomotive barked her way up the gradients, not stopping at the soon-to-be closed stations (six months later) of Thornhill and Sanquhar, before breasting the summit at Polquhap Sidings (620ft) prior to 20 miles of descent into Kilmarnock. The scenery then changed from thick-forested slopes to a wide-open, somewhat desolate vista with fewer trees in evidence. Why this train ran I am unable to remember – was it a mail or paper train? Whatever the purpose, it was, amongst so many early morning journeys undertaken during the 1960s, an unforgettable experience. It should be noted that, along with a great many blinkered decisions in respect of line or station closures made back then, Sanquhar, New Cumnock and Auchinleck have all been subsequently reopened.

At Kilmarnock the Black 5MT took the front vans off and placed them in a bay platform, leaving the truncated portion to be worked forward by Hurlford's Standard 4MTT 80111. The line I was now travelling over originally opened as a 'plateway' in 1812 but was reconstructed to main-line standards in 1841. Twenty-seven locomotives were allocated to Hurlford (67B), a shed located adjacent to the G&SWR main line over a mile south of Kilmarnock, including 30 per cent of the twenty strong 77xxx BR Standard 2MT class. Due to the late running I had to bale out at Troon – a location renowned throughout the golfing world – in order to regain my planned schedule to head for Glasgow. Some of the Ayr–Kilmarnock trains were steam operated (I read afterwards!), but alas not the one I was to travel on that morning – a mundane 'bog cart'! Several weeks later, a print of a photograph I took at Kilmarnock of Kingmoor's Black 5 44802 storming through on a relief ex London revealed one, perhaps about to work a train, loitering at the south end of the station.

I had now returned to my planned itinerary and a pleasing catch of Corkerhill's lifelong (eleven years, two months) resident Standard 5MT 73102 on a G&SWR-routed stopping service from Annan, taking me into Glasgow

On Saturday 24 July 1965 I had originally planned to go through to Ayr on the 03.21 from Carlisle but due to late running I was only able to make it to Troon; my return train to Kilmarnock can be seen approaching! Hurlford's Standard 4MT 80111, which had taken over at Kilmarnock, was to be transferred to Beattock the following year, and was later withdrawn in December 1966.

At Kilmarnock Kingmoor's 44802 storms through with an overnight relief from Euston to Glasgow. One of the luckier locomotives to escape the massacre upon the shed's closure in December 1967, she was transferred to Bolton, being withdrawn in June 1968.

St Enoch, went some way to improve my demeanour. This was my fifteenth Standard 5MT (of an eventual seventy-seven) and, in my opinion, with their high running plates, they made for one of the more handsome designs of steam locomotive.

When opened in 1850, this former G&SWR route between Gretna Junction and Glasgow – the line over which I was now travelling – then terminated at Glasgow's Bridge Street station on the south bank of the River Clyde. Both the G&SWR and the Caledonian Railway were prevented from crossing the Clyde by an assortment of organisations, the main one being the Glasgow Corporation, all insisting that any bridge crossing the Clyde must contain at least one lifting section. Eventually in 1876 the G&SWR thwarted this opposition by constructing an alternative route to the city diverging from West Street via the Gorbals, crossing the Clyde on an impressive castellated bridge at Hutchesontown into the terminus of St Enoch, which became their headquarters. Only three years later the Bridge Street station was rebuilt to provide through platforms to cross the Clyde into Glasgow Central, which the rival CR used.

St Enoch station, located adjacent to the same named square, dispatched train services to most parts of the G&SWR system, including Ayr, Stranraer, Carlisle and, in partnership with the Midland Railway, to Leeds, Sheffield and London St Pancras via Ais Gill. The station was the first public building in Glasgow to be lit by electricity and in 1901 was doubled in size to twelve platforms. Although provided with two impressive semi-cylindrical glass- and iron-roofed train sheds, by the time of my visit the station had a neglected, underused atmosphere. This intentionally under-maintained scenario, frequently associated with locations destined for obliteration, was often encountered during my travels in the 1960s under the guise of financial expenditure avoidance. Sure enough the station was closed to passengers on 27 June 1966 (and to parcels a year later) as part of the rationalisation of the railway system undertaken by Dr Beeching. Upon closure its 250 trains and 23,000 passengers a day were diverted to Glasgow Central. The roofs of the structure were demolished, despite protests, in 1977 and although the entire site was razed at least the station clock was saved – and can now be seen in Cumbernauld town centre.

Glasgow, 50 miles from the sea, is the third-largest city in the UK. Crossed by twenty-one bridges, the River Clyde, which effectively splits the city in two, was its lifeblood over the years, spawning numerous dockyards at which a great many ships were built. The industrial revolution with its attendant skills in manufacturing, textiles and engineering gave rise to a rapid increase in population predominantly housed in myriad tenement blocks. In the 1960s the Bruce report set out a series of initiatives to turn around the decline in standards of living suffered by the occupants of the tenements, recommending they be demolished and the inhabitants be relocated to the burgeoning suburbs surrounding the city. Recent accolades such as being selected to host the Commonwealth Games in 2014 show matters have certainly improved over the years. As for famous personages having been born there, the list is endless. Perhaps just three (still with us at the time of writing) are worthy of a mention: football player and manager Sir Alex Ferguson, comedian, musician and actor Billy Connolly, and singer, actress and TV personality Marie Lawrie (Lulu).

Back to 1965 and having passed through the southern suburbs on the previous visit, I had never set foot in Glasgow before and needed to find the former North British Railway's Queen Street station in order to continue my itinerary en route to the Fife coast. This was never a problem – providing I had in my possession my *British Locomotive Shed Directory* which not only gave detailed instructions as to how to get to all the motive-power depots throughout Britain but, rather conveniently, published street maps of all the major cities.

Queen Street station was built by the Edinburgh & Glasgow Railway and opened on 21 February 1842. In 1865 the E&GR was absorbed into the North British Railway, which became part of the LNER group in 1923. All trains departing the station have to surmount the 2,090-yard-long Cowlairs incline, 1,000 yards of which is in a tunnel and on a rising gradient as steep as 1 in 42 in places. Trains were initially hauled up on a rope operated by a stationary engine but following a series of accidents banking locomotives were used from 1908.

Queen Street station's platforms are on two levels, with the High Level platforms running directly north–south, and the Low Level running east–west. The High Level station is the larger of the two levels and is the terminus for the Edinburgh shuttles and all routes north of the central belt. Platforms 1–7 occupy the High Level, Platform 1 being at the western end of the train shed, and being considerably shorter – it is usually only used for local stopping services. Platforms 8 and 9 comprise the Low Level station, and it is the most central stop on the North Clyde Line of the Glasgow suburban electric network. The Low Level line between High Street, Queen Street and Charing Cross was built before the Glasgow Subway, making it the oldest underground railway in the city. Reconstruction work has begun (involving a twenty-week-long closure during 2016) to make Queen Street Scotland's third busiest station: a 'world-class transport hub'. As the tunnel at the north end of the site restricts any extension that way, the platforms can only be lengthened to accommodate longer trains southwards. This will dramatically alter the concourse layout, by default providing a two-level passenger circulating area together with a modern glass frontage.

The train most crucial to this 1965 visit was the 09.40 from here to St Andrews. With steam locomotives yet to be banned from Queen Street (the eventual ban coming in November 1966 congruent with the closure of Buchanan Street), I was disappointed, but not surprised, for the train to be a DMU – although it would have been an understatement to say I would have preferred a loco-hauled DL resourced train for the 3½-hour 103-mile journey ahead! After making daylight at the top of Cowlairs incline, Eastfield (65A) depot was passed, it retaining just a handful of steam locomotives, mainly B1s, at what was now a predominantly diesel depot. I did note, however, St Rollox's sole A4 60031 *Golden Plover* in the area. The train I was travelling on only ran for eight Saturdays that summer and, having called at Falkirk High, Polmont, Linlithgow and Dalmeny, it took me on my first trip over the impressive the then 75-year-old Forth Railway Bridge.

Taking seven years to build, with a loss of over seventy men, the bridge was officially opened by the Prince of Wales (later King Edward VII) in 1890. The total length of the complete bridge is just over 1½ miles and the three great 361ft-high tower cantilevers rest on granite piers all linked with metal supports somewhat indicative of a spider's web. Train speeds are limited to 50mph for passenger and 20mph for freight services. Although once a well-used colloquial expression, the phrase 'like painting the Forth Bridge' (i.e. a never-ending job) was never factually accurate, according to a 2004 *New Civil Engineering* report; nevertheless both under BR and its predecessors the bridge always had a permanent maintenance crew based there. In July 2015 UNESCO designated the bridge as a World Heritage Site and there are plans afoot to add a visitor centre and viewing platform to it.

Back to 1965 and onwards we went, via Inverkeithing, Dunfermline and Cowdenbeath, before arriving at the diverging station for the Fife Coast line – Thornton Junction. The majority of passenger services over the line I had just travelled were truncated at Cardenden in 1969, and Thornton Junction station itself was closed. As with many of the service withdrawals during the 1960s, it was another example of the short-sightedness that then prevailed within BR management and, in 1989, the line was reopened as part of 'The Fife Circle' – a loop-line service based on Edinburgh. Three years later, a short distance away from the original Thornton Junction, a new station built to serve the growing township of Glenrothes was opened.

Thornton Junction (62A) shed was the beating heart of the Fife coalfield and, being ex LNER territory, several more classes of steam locomotives I had

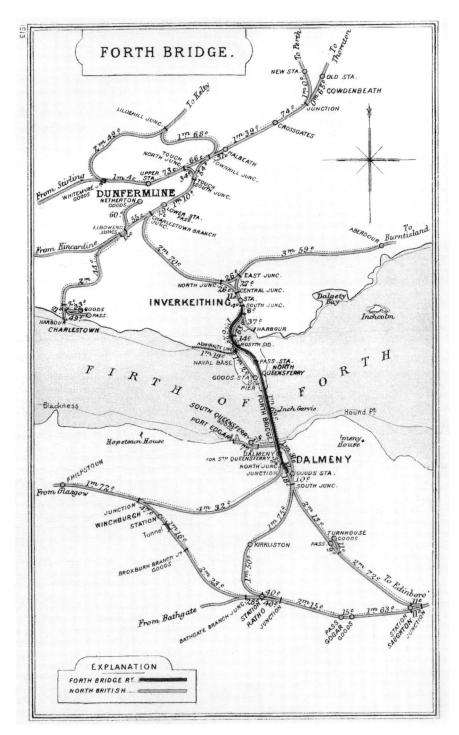

A 1913 Railway Clearing House map of the Forth Bridge and associated rail routes. (Railway Junction Diagram, Wikimedia Commons)

never witnessed before were noted. It was like stepping into a time warp, being surrounded by archaic tall-chimney old-timers from a past life! The allocation of thirty-eight locomotives comprised four 4-6-0 B1s for passenger services together with eight 51-year-old 0-6-0 J37s, two 77-year-old 0-6-0 J36s, eleven 39-year-old 0-6-0 J38s and eleven WD 2-8-0s for dealing with the extensive freight requirements. This ex NBR shed was one of the final seven to close in May 1967. So at last, after 2 hours of fume-filled rattling, we went on to the Fife Coast branch. This coastal route via Leven, Largo, Anstruther, Crail and St Andrews was one of the last lines opened in Scotland – in 1887. Presumably only covering its running costs during the short summer season, the 28-mile section between Leven and St Andrews was to be closed in September 1965. This left a 'stub' at each end – but not for long. The St Andrews–Leuchars Junction section closed in January 1969, and the Thornton Junction–Leven section (to passengers) the following October. There is a scheme for the latter closure to be reinstated but, as always, costs appear to have stalled the plans which are currently mothballed.

This wonderfully scenic line weaved in and out of the many sandy-beached Fife coast resorts often paralleling the coast itself. With ancient fishing villages, historic castles and famous golf courses, the only down side is the often fierce wind coming off the North Sea. With only five trains (all DMUs) a day serving the section north of Crail, to say I was exasperated would be an understatement as I witnessed *all* other trains, mostly summer Saturday short-dated services between Crail and Edinburgh, crossed on the single-tracked route as being steam (B1) operated. When viewing passenger services being operated by classes of steam locomotives I had yet to be hauled by, the 'must return one day' scenario kicks in, and, as readers will progress to in the following chapter, I saw to the matter quickly!

I stretched my legs during the 17-minute connection at St Andrews, a town once described rather disparagingly by visiting English writer Samuel (Dr) Johnson in 1773: 'one of its streets is now lost; and in those that remain there is the silence and solitude of inactive indigence and gloomy de-population.' But it is now world-renowned for its Royal and Ancient Golf Club. I then boarded the same DMU for the 10-minute journey to the ECML junction station at Leuchars, changing there for a Dundee-bound train that would take me over the Tay Bridge – Scotland's second most impressive rail bridge crossing.

Opened in 1878, the original 2-mile-long Tay Bridge, built to supersede the Tayport ferry, collapsed the following year while a train was crossing. Subsequent investigation revealed a catalogue of errors during its construction including poor design, inadequate preparation and downright bad workmanship. The

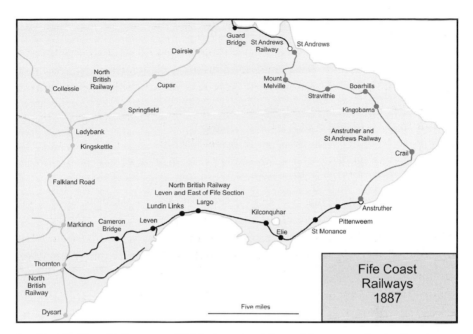

An 1887 Fife Coast Railway map. (© Afterbrunel and licensed for reuse under the Creative Commons Licence)

The weather had deteriorated by the time I reached eastern Scotland, where I had my first sighting of a Thompson-designed B1. Here, at Thornton Junction on Saturday 24 July 1965, home-allocated B1 4-6-0 61148 is caught shunting her two-coach set for the 12.03 Crail departure.

The only J38 0-6-0 I witnessed was Thornton Junction's 65922. As the poor-quality shot taken from my passing DMU was not considered good enough for publication, here, at the same location, on Sunday 16 October 1966, her withdrawn sister 65907 heads a line-up of other condemned locomotives (61132, 61350, 90160 & 90600). (Keith Lawrence)

It seemed as if all trains along the Fife Coast line (other than mine!) were B1 operated. Being single-tracked most stations were crossing points and here, at Anstruther, the 12.30 Crail–Edinburgh Waverley with lifelong Dundee resident 61102 is captured by camera by leaning out of my DMU's window.

replacement eighty-five-span bridge, built 60ft upstream, over which I travelled that day, was opened in 1887; the piers of the original are still in situ alongside. I spied Dundee (62B) shed just prior to descending to the somewhat cramped island platform station of Dundee Tay Bridge, Dundee's other station, that of the West, having closed just months earlier.

Dundee, Scotland's fourth-largest city and the one-time capital of Forfarshire, has been awarded the sobriquet of 'yes city', being one of just four constituencies to vote for Scottish independence in 2014's referendum. Staying with politics, the following year the Scottish National Party (SNP) collected a landslide fifty-six seats (out of a possible fifty-nine) in the May General Election. Back to 1965 and, although fully expectant that the next train I was to catch would be yet another DMU, at least there were a couple of steam photographic opportunities during the hour's wait. Although failing, for whatever reason, to take one of Ferryhill and subsequently preserved allocated A4 60009 *Union of South Africa* when calling for water and a crew change while working a troop special from Scarborough to Aberdeen, I was more successful in capturing one of Reid's 51-year-old J37s, 64608, which was pottering around with some wagons. The comparison between the two couldn't have been more stark: the sleek lines of one of Gresley's streamlined Pacifics compared to one of Reid's antiquated tall-chimney veterans.

As an aside, while researching for this book I found out that an hour after my departure from Dundee one of the two remaining A3s, 60052 *Prince Palatine*

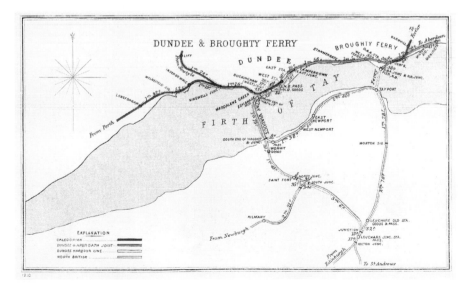

A 1910 Railway Clearing House map of the Tay Bridge and associated rail routes. (Railway Junction Diagram, Wikimedia Commons)

One of 62B's stud of nine 0-6-0 J37s, 46-year-old Reid-designed 64608, is seen passing through Dundee Tay Bridge station on Saturday 24 July 1965 with a short freight. She was just weeks away from her demise.

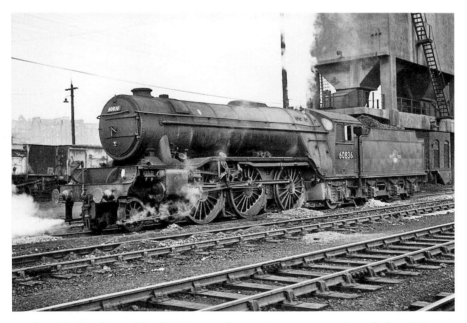

My first sighting of one of Gresley's V2 2-6-2 locomotives, 60836, was through the window of my DMU when passing Dundee shed. Here, in precisely the same position, she is seen on Sunday 16 October 1966. This Darlington-built 26-year-old was destined to become the final Scottish example of the class, being withdrawn at the end of December 1966. (Keith Lawrence)

(64A), arrived with the 14.25 from Edinburgh, which although was terminating there had called at Leuchars Junction an hour after I had left. Just as well I wasn't aware of it back then – I wouldn't have been a happy bunny! I was once again about to pass 62B and, given its allocation of twenty-nine locomotives mostly of LNER lineage, I attempted, by hanging out of the train's window, to take what turned out to be poor-quality blurred shots – most of them not good enough to be published here. Whilst the B1s (ten) predominated, there were also nine J37s and most importantly, from a steam passenger haulage enthusiast's point of view, three 4-6-2 A2s and five 2-6-2 V2s. The allocation of the Pacifics gave the shed a certain kudos and, although nearly always tantalisingly on view, they were only dispatched, together with the V2s, out on the main line to work fully fitted freight or short-notice replacements for DL failures on passenger services. What chance did an enthusiast living over 400 miles away have of obtaining a run with one? Although highly unlikely, there was no harm in trying – and try I did, as the reader will discover further into the book.

That warm July afternoon I was heading for Perth in order to connect into the same train as on my previous visit, 'The Grampian', in the hope of a second A4 catch. Sure enough, just minutes after arrival following a frustrating steamless 7 hours, Ferryhill's A4 60007 *Sir Nigel Gresley* arrived bang on time with her 15.50 six-coach departure for Glasgow.

The succeeding Caledonian Railway expanded Perth General railway station in 1884; originally designed by William Tite, it was opened in 1848 by the Scottish Central Railway. The expansion in part was to accommodate two extra platforms serving Dundee-bound trains, which upon heading east had to negotiate a tightly curved single-track bridge straddling the River Tay. Rationalisation due to the reduction in train services concurrent with the closure of the Forfar 'cut-off' portion in 1967, coupled with necessary extensive repairs to the high overall roof and the discovery of dry rot in the east side buildings, led to two of the original through lines being truncated. By default, the Dundee corridor platforms became the most heavily utilised platforms and as such have undergone refurbishment, making them the central point of the station. Once provided with an impressive frontage, this expansive station has undergone considerable alteration over the years, and not necessarily to its aesthetic benefit – the most recent, a footbridge between platforms to meet disability legislation, has been described as a 'carbuncle desecrating the Victorian station environment'.

This was all former Caledonian Railway territory and Perth shed (63A), passed immediately upon departure, reflected this. Instead of representatives of LNER classes, as witnessed earlier that day, the origins were of pure LMS – out

Having arrived into Glasgow's Buchanan Street on 'The Grampian' at 17.30, I raced to the north end of the station to photograph A4 60024 *Kingfisher* departing with the simultaneously timed departure of 'The St Mungo' – a service named after the patron saint of Glasgow.

Doncaster-built 28-year-old LNER A4 4-6-2 60007 *Sir Nigel Gresley* resting at the buffer stops at Glasgow's Buchanan Street station having worked in on the 13.30 'The Grampian' from Aberdeen. She was to be withdrawn just seven months later into a life of preservation.

of an allocation of thirty the majority (twenty-six) were Black 5s. This shed was to survive several months beyond the end of Scottish steam purely to service Kingmoor's locomotives continuing to be sent over the border. Having said that, a surprising 'cop' (if my notes made at the time were accurate) of withdrawn Thompson A2 60512 *Steady Aim* was jotted down – or could that have been at her home shed of Dundee?

The enthusiasm of *Sir Nigel Gresley's* crew shone through during that 63½-mile journey with heavy usage of the distinctive chime whistle, smart station dwell times and some exhilarating running. All too soon I was arriving into Glasgow's Buchanan Street station witnessing sister A4 60024 *Kingfisher* departing with the annoyingly simultaneous (17.30) 'St Mungo' departure. In just two visits to Scotland I had 'copped' seven out of ten A4s there.

This was the third Glasgow terminus that I had visited that day – with just the Central station yet to be travelled into. Glasgow Buchanan Street was opened in 1849 as the CR's main terminus for the city. Initially comprising of just two platforms in 1932, the LMS rebuilt the station, trebling the number of platforms, equipping the frontage with a steel-framed structure clad in horizontal timber boarding, mock columns, pilasters, a pronounced cornice, a small tower and a glazed canopy supported by two iron columns. In comparison, however, to the neighbouring Queen Street and imposing Central and St Enoch stations it seemed a drab and uninspiring building, remaining basically unchanged until closure. There was never an overall roof or train shed – just a glass-roofed concourse and awnings over the platforms; even they were second-hand, having come from the closed Ardrossan North station. The station was earmarked for closure and replacement in the Bruce report – a set of proposals whose aim was to redevelop Glasgow in the post-Second World War period. The plan included replacing Buchanan Street and Queen Street stations with a Glasgow North station on land including the site of Buchanan Street, but many times larger. There was also a similar scheme to replace Central and St Enoch stations with a Glasgow South station, but neither came to fruition. Despite this reprieve, it proved only to be temporary as the station was closed in November 1966 as part of the streamlining of the railway system, with most of its services diverted to Queen Street. Although the station and adjacent goods yard were soon demolished, Glasgow's principal bus station was developed on the former whilst the new headquarters for BR Scottish Region (Buchanan House) was constructed on the latter.

I was to return east on the 18.15 Dundee departure to Perth that evening with another of St Rollox's Caprotti Standard 5s 73150. Boy what a difference in noise! Although already highlighted in Chapter 1, when describing my first

Apologies to the publishers but I simply had to include this, my only shot of a BR Clan Pacific locomotive. Lifelong Kingmoor resident 72008 *Clan Macleod* is seen at Perth at the head of the 20.25 Marylebone departure. She was one of only two, out of a class of ten, to survive into 1966, being withdrawn the following April. Plans are well advanced, at the time of writing, with the new construction of 72010 *Hengist*.

departure from Buchanan Street, I feel compelled to repeat the scene I was witnessing once more. Instead of the quietly efficient emission associated with the Gresley locomotives, Riddles Standard 5MTs, in the hands of the seemingly gung-ho St Rollox crews, were renowned for their fierce exhalation of exhaust on these semis. As she stormed up the 3-mile 1 in 79/98 climb to Robroyston, and indeed all the way on the route to Perth, I can still imagine the acoustic, visual and, dare I say it, emotional effect it had on me. With her trajectory of smoke shooting high into the atmosphere, the resultant noise reverberating off the surrounding hills, this was what I was careering around the country for!

The final 'new' class to be seen that day, at Perth shed, was one of the four remaining BR Standard 6P5F 4-6-2 Clans – 72008 *Clan Macleod*. Ten of these Standard Class 6 locomotives were constructed during the years 1951–52, a further fifteen being initially delayed by acute shortage of steel in Britain and eventually cancelled altogether upon publication of the 1955 Modernisation Plan. They were designed to be a lighter alternative to their big Britannia sisters but received mixed reception from crews due to their inability to maintain the Class 1 passenger schedules they were often rostered for. The Scottish Region had withdrawn their examples of the class – *Clan Macleod*, together with the remaining three, being allocated to Kingmoor.

I had returned to Perth to catch my final train of the weekend – the 20.25 Perth–Marylebone. This summer-dated train had, on SX days only, through sleepers and carriages from Oban, which were attached at Stirling during its call there from 21.09 to 21.30. Further time was 'lost' at Carstairs (22.50 to 23.24) for a portion from Glasgow Central, which had departed there at 22.20 and had to bypass us while standing in the platform prior to reversing on to the front. Not being depicted as steam operated within my *Scottish Railfans* book, to say I was delighted upon seeing a steam locomotive backing down would be an understatement. That was good enough but upon realising it was *Clan Macleod* herself my delight became euphoric! Naively unaware of the aforementioned Carstairs shunting arrangements, I fully expected to be taken over Beattock by her but alas the Glasgow portion's power, in the form of Type 2 D5348 (Class 27), took us forward.

After crossing the border this Anglo-Scottish train called at Carlisle (01.00) to change traction to a Type 4 DL, at Crewe (04.25) for an AC Electric change and at Rugby (05.45) for further haulage by another Type 4. On days other than Sundays it would arrive into Euston at 07.25 but on Sunday mornings, resulting from the ongoing WCML electrification work south of Rugby, it was sched-uled to run via Northampton, Blisworth, the Bletchley flyover, Claydon LNE Junction then up the ex GCR via Wendover to Marylebone due in at 08.20. Having had a decent night's kip, stretched out in a compartment to myself, without having to worry about alighting anywhere on route, by the time the Chilterns went by a fully awake and refreshed enthusiast was able to enjoy the delights of the sunlit countryside and suburbs prior to the population arising – on this particular occasion enhanced by the sighting of London Transport's ex GWR pannier tank, the subsequently preserved L95, on an engineering train at Aylesbury. That 464-mile journey contributed to the weekend's mile-age total of 1,113 during which I had witnessed many previously unobserved classes of steam locomotives, travelled over miles of new (to me) track, some of which were to succumb to closure within months, and passed by and viewed a further six steam sheds. I promised myself a return trip north of the border in two weeks' time – I couldn't wait!

5

STEAM HAULED OVER THE FIRTHS

WE NOW MOVE on to August 1965 and to set the scene we start off with some non-railway news of that month. Cigarette advertising was banned on British TV (cigars and pipe tobacco remained until 1991), Jim Clark won the German Grand Prix and boxer Muhammad Ali attracted extensively media coverage while on his first visit to Scotland with his lyrical passage as follows:

I'd heard of a man named Burns – supposed to be a poet
But if he was how come I didn't know it
They told me his work was very very neat
So I replied 'But who did he beat'.

Musically, The Beatles had taken the top chart position with 'Help', from their recently released film.

The largest table, sixty-five pages in fact, within the 832-page LMR summer issue that year was Table 50, which showed all services over the WCML from London Euston to Carlisle. If the traveller happened to have turned to p. 120 they would have seen a 19.20 wavy-lined departure above which the letters G and FO together with the symbols depicting a cup of tea and a bed were shown. This Fridays Only train operated until 27 August and conveyed a miniature buffet car to Preston, sleepers and through carriages from London to Oban and at Wigan North Western they attached through carriages from Manchester Exchange to Perth. Just three weeks prior to its cessation, on Friday the 6th, I boarded the train for another expedition to Scotland – presumably, as I was destined for Perth, having to move carriages en route.

The journey that night was to provide a catalogue of adversities! It had a 16-minute delayed start because of the late arrival into Euston of the ECS, an extra 10 minutes waiting at Crewe for the Crewe North foreman to dispatch Brit 70020 *Mercury* out for the train, much longer than the scheduled 9 minutes at Wigan North Western for the Manchester portion to be attached and took what seemed like forever and a day to climb both Shap and Beattock banks – in both cases the lengthy train requiring assistance. We had exchanged Brits at Carlisle, with 70033 *Charles Dickens* working forward and, taking into consideration that dawn was breaking when ascending Beattock, if it wasn't for concerns in connection with the day's planned itinerary being thrown into chaos, I would have enjoyed yet another barnstorming early morning entry into the glorious countryside southern Scotland has to offer. After the Oban portion had been detached at Stirling, although relishing over 290 steam-hauled miles north of Crewe, the eventual 91-minute late arrival into Perth at 07.01 did in fact completely kibosh my intended plan to travel forward to Aberdeen on the 06.35 departure (04.05 ex Glasgow Buchanan Street), though annoyingly I saw the train disappearing into the distance itself over half an hour late!

After finding a nearby station seat, out came the ever-present, now decidedly dog-eared, timetable and, with a drink – allegedly tea – from the station buffet, I set about rearranging my day's activities. My original plan was, having travelled to Aberdeen via Forfar, to return south over the ECML on either the 08.45 or 09.10 departures – both services shown in the timetable with a wavy line through the timings column. These short-dated summer Saturday-only trains were exactly the ones that steam were most likely to work and in order to intercept them I formulated a revised itinerary, which meant that by travelling on an 08.00 DMU via Dundee I would join them further into their journeys at Arbroath.

So after taking a photograph of the 07.15 departure, a train that would have stranded me at Aberdeen for several steamless hours had I travelled on it, with Perth's Black 5 44797 I caught the DMU to Arbroath – a town originally known as Aberbrothock so named after the Brothock Burn that runs through the town, and whose football team had ended the previous season languishing in the middle of the Second Division. The nearby Arbroath Abbey was the setting of the first declaration of Scottish independence in 1320, which was sealed by fifty-one magnates and nobles. Arbroath's other claim to fame is the 'smokie' – haddock smoked over hardwood using a special process – and visitors are able to follow a smokie trail.

Disappointingly Type 4 D361 (Class 40) turned up with the first of the two dated services and why I caught it to Dundee rather than await the following one, a mere 27 minutes later, I shall never know – but that's what my tattered

Perth's Black 5 44797 makes a vigorous start with the 07.15, all stations via Forfar, departure for Aberdeen on Saturday 7 August 1965. This lifelong (nineteen years) resident of 63A was withdrawn in September 1966 and the former Caledonian route via Forfar closed a year later.

Ferryhill's A4 60026 *Miles Beevor*, another King's Cross refugee, pauses at Dundee Tay Bridge with the 09.10 summer Saturdays-only Aberdeen–Edinburgh Waverley. For the first ten years of her life she had carried the name *Kestrel*.

notebook shows. The only way to communicate to other enthusiasts back then as to what was steam and what was not was via the grapevine and one of my friends had said that a fortnight previously an A4 had worked the following 09.10 ex Aberdeen.

Lady Luck was to be with me that day because not only was it steam powered but with an A4 to boot. Long-term King's Cross, now Ferryhill, resident 60026 *Miles Beevor* was working the train that Saturday and, although as always hoping for an elusive V2, my third A4 was a more than welcome substitute. Looking and sounding in quite bad condition, it came as no surprise to learn she was withdrawn later that year. With numbers now down to eight, I considered this catch quite a coup and, after passing the Dundee shed and witnessing A2 60530 *Sayajirao* in light steam on standby duty, I settled down for my 60-mile journey south. Routed via the Tay Bridge, Cupar, Kirkcaldy and the Forth Bridge, a thoroughly enjoyable 2-hour journey, fuelled with half-melted Club biscuits and day-old partially crushed sandwiches, was enjoyed, the sunny weather contributing to the happiness factor.

Readers may recall, during the previous chapter, that LNER Thompson B1 locomotives powered a great many Fife Coast services – a class I had yet to obtain runs behind. Having spent many hours poring over the Scottish Region timetable during the intervening period, I had deliberately engineered this visit's schedule in order to travel on two of them. All right, you might say,

Taken from a passing train, one of the three remaining A2s, Peppercorn-designed 60530 *Sayajirao*, is on standby duty at Dundee shed. Only being utilised on fully fitted freights or failure substitutions on Class 1 passenger services, she escaped my clutches, being withdrawn in November 1966.

the distance wasn't great: Edinburgh to Inverkeithing and back was a mere
13¼ miles each way, but beggars can't be choosers. Crossing the Forth Bridge
three times in one day aboard increasingly rare steam-operated passenger services was, to me, a result.

My train home was always going to be the 20.25 ex Perth and so I made
my way over from Edinburgh to the ex CR main line on the 16.24 DMU to
Stirling. Routed via Dunfermline, Oakley and Alloa, yet another steam shed
was passed – 62C Dunfermline. With an allocation of nearly thirty, the largest
classes being eleven J38s and seven WDs, this Fife coalfield shed, which was one
of the last ones to close, could be easily viewed from the train when calling at
Dunfermline Upper station.

The Stirling & Dunfermline Railway opened this line in 1850 but only as
far as the administrative town of Alloa, Clackmannanshire, with passengers
for Stirling completing their journey by ferry along the River Forth. This
situation persisted until the line through to Stirling was opened two years
later – the terminus, however, for the town was to the north of the Forth. In
July 1853, a bridge across the Forth was built and the line was extended to the
Scottish Central Railway station. Even though it was not included within the
Beeching proposals for closure, the entire 20-mile-long line was deemed sufficiently uneconomic, and BR withdrew passenger services in October 1968.
This move was another example of short-sightedness that prevailed within

Steam at Edinburgh Waverley in the form of Thornton Junction's B1 61133 awaiting departure
time with the 13.18 summer Saturdays-only train for Crail. This was to be the final year of
regular B1-operated passenger services within Scotland – and indeed the Fife Coast line itself.

Spending most of her early years at Glasgow's Eastfield shed before briefly calling in at Corkerhill and Ayr, B1 61396's final shed was to be St Margarets. Seen here passing through Inverkeithing with a southbound freight, she was withdrawn just four weeks later.

The train I had passed at Anstruther two weeks previously, the 12.30 Crail–Edinburgh Waverley, arrives at Inverkeithing with 62A's Gorton-built Thompson-designed B1 61343 in charge.

the retrenchment-minded BR because, due to an increasing population, Alloa station, although resited due to the construction of a leisure centre, was reconnected to the passenger National Network at Stirling in May 2008; the majority of the east section formed the West Fife Way cycle path.

Until 1930 there was a second Forth-hugging railway between Alloa and Dunfermline. This was reopened to freight in 1997 for traffic to Kincardine power station and the Longannet Fly Ash plant; subject to the necessary funding, it might one day reopen to passengers as well.

So now I was in situ at Stirling to catch any one of three trains, having noted them all over the previous two visits as being steam operated, to travel 33 miles north to Perth. I didn't have to wait long because the first of them, the 17.30 'St Mungo' from Glasgow Buchanan Street to Aberdeen, was worked that evening by A4 60009 *Union of South Africa*. This subsequently preserved A4, a lifelong Scottish resident, had her 15 minutes of fame throughout the world in 2015 when working the Royal Train over the reopened Borders Line between Edinburgh and Tweedbank. Aboard the Royal Train on that September day was Queen Elizabeth II who was celebrating becoming the longest reigning British monarch – exceeding Queen Victoria's sixty-three years and 216 days.

I shall never forget, having travelled overnight down from London and been on the go all day in Scotland, the sense of satisfaction upon boarding the 20.25 Perth departure. The train was usually formed of LMS vehicles and was lightly loaded passenger-wise, so I selected a compartment close to the locomotive, took my shoes off, finished off whatever food I had left, stretched out lengthways and looked out at the beautiful scenery (the Scottish summer days seemed to last forever) passing by. After a long day bashing it was a relief not to having to concern myself about staying awake or missing onward connections should fatigue take over! Having had a Clan on the train two weeks previously, perhaps I was expecting too much and, although 'mundane' Black 5, 45120, took me the 77 miles south to Carstairs, the Glasgow portion to which we were attached (DL hauled two weeks previously) turning up with Leeds Holbeck-allocated Jubilee 45593 *Kolhapur* – yet another class I had never travelled with being scratched! Down to just thirty Jubilee-class locomotives remaining throughout the country, she was the first, of an eventual twelve, members of the once-prolific class I was to catch runs with. The routing of this overnight train from Claydon LNER Junction via Grendon Underwood Junction and Princes Risborough led to a 14-minute late arrival into Marylebone at 08.34. At 1,120 miles, this had been my lengthiest journey yet (just) – but having successfully achieved steam over both Firth bridges, two further catches of Gresley's A4s and two new classes (B1 and Jubilee), I wasn't complaining.

6

MIXED FORTUNES

THIS, MY FINAL Scottish visit of 1965, was made with two objectives in mind. Having so far failed to obtain a run with one of the dozen remaining V2s or travel into Aberdeen with steam, I was intent on remedying these matters once and for all. We haulage aficionados in those days always perused each region's weekly STNs specifically for relief services, knowing that there was always a greater chance of steam power operating them. It was Friday 20 August and musically The Rolling Stones had released what was to become their first chart-topping success in the USA, 'Satisfaction', whilst here Sonny & Cher had a number-one hit with their 'I Got You Babe'.

I had boarded the 19.02 Inverness-bound relief departure out of Euston that evening. All went well to Crewe, where Brit 70052 *Firth of Tay* took over for the 141-mile journey over Shap to Carlisle. Losing time en route (Brit 52 not very well?), we were looped at Penrith (for 'The Royal Highlander' to pass), eventually staggering into Carlisle over an hour late. Was it just me or did it appear that both signalmen and motive-power foremen treat such extras with a certain disdain – these 'low-priority' trains being routed via slow lines wherever feasible and resourced with inferior-conditioned locomotives?

Upon arriving into Carlisle I was sorely tempted to throw my plans out of the window because one of the by then four surviving Clans, a required 72007 *Clan Mackintosh*, was waiting to take the 19.20 Euston–Perth onwards. Perhaps, in those early days of my travels, I lacked the confidence to veer away from my pre-planned itinerary. Besides which, I can only assume after all these years, the priority was to reach Aberdeen that day and my train *should* have preceded it! With yet another required locomotive, Brit 70035 *Thomas Hardy*, waiting to

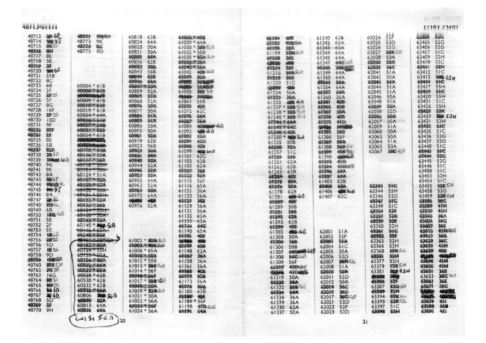

An extract from the autumn 1965 *Locoshed* book. These pages required updating every month with information gleaned from either the LCGB bulletin or the 'Motive Power Miscellany' section of *The Railway World* magazine. The blanked-out entries denote that the locomotive has been withdrawn; the right-sided amendment signifies that she has moved sheds and the lined entry indicates that I have had a run with her.

take 'The Northern Irishman' forward, where was our steed? Those two trains came and went, and eventually a sorry-looking 12A Black 5, 44802, leaked into view, allegedly fit enough to take my thirteen-coach train over the undulating gradients into Scotland! Needless to say, even with a banker up Beattock, we lost more time and after exchanging Black 5s at Carstairs eventually arrived into Perth 198 minutes late at 07.48.

In a similar scenario to the one encountered two weeks previously, I had planned to travel forward to Aberdeen on the 06.35 departure – a 2-hour connection being considered adequate! Now I had even missed the 07.15 stopper as well and so, once again, I found myself heading to Arbroath on the 08.00 DMU via Dundee service. The time spent there passed pleasantly enough witnessing Dundee's solitary Ivatt Mogul 46464 playing with some wagons out of the Metal Box Sidings on the former Carmyllie branch. As befitting a depot 'pet', she was polished to perfection. She was withdrawn in December 1966, initially being privately purchased and presented to Dundee City Corporation for display as a static exhibit. Following her 15 minutes of fame when working the first public

With nameplates already removed to thwart souvenir hunters, 70036 *Boadicea* slowly emerges out of the early morning mist at Stirling on Saturday 24 August 1965 with a southbound troop train. Starting life at Stratford working express services out of Liverpool Street, she was withdrawn at Kingmoor in October 1966.

Dundee's 'pet' LMS Mogul; Crewe-built Ivatt-designed 15-year-old 46464 shunts wagons at Arbroath having worked the morning Carmyllie branch freight. Although withdrawn in September the following year, she has survived into preservation.

train over the Strathspey Railway metals in July 1978, she is now awaiting restoration near the CR's Bridge of Dun station.

It was the last timetabled day of the 10.34 departure for Edinburgh (09.10 ex Aberdeen) and it was one of those euphoric moments every chaser deserves once in a while when seeing my fifth (out of eight, don't forget!) catch of an A4, 60024 *Kingfisher*, working the train that sunny morning. Only travelling the short distance over the Tay Bridge to Leuchars Junction, I noted, when passing by Dundee shed, three visiting locomotives: J38 65915 (62A), A4 60031 *Golden Plover* (65B) and Brit 70038 *Robin Hood* (12A). Alas, the A4 had only weeks to live. Home-allocated V2 60836 and A2 60530 *Sayajirao*, both in light steam and presumably on standby duties, were also tantalisingly on view. I had alighted at Leuchars Junction to return north back over the Tay Bridge on the 10.30 Edinburgh–Aberdeen service – a sometimes-reported V2 working. What did I get? Perth's Black 5 44704! Was I ever going to travel with a V2 like most of my travelling colleagues?

With all the anticipated morning V2 workings failing to materialise, I then returned to my planned itinerary which was to travel over the sparsely served (threatened with closure) Throsk Bridge branch that connected Alloa with Larbert. With time to kill at Dundee, I made a fill-in DMU journey over the Tayport branch.

The first railway to reach Tayport was from the south, at Leuchars, and was opened in 1850. Until the building of the Tay Bridge, this line was the only

Perth's Black 5 Horwich-built 17-year-old 44704 leads the 10.30 Edinburgh Waverley to Aberdeen over the Tay Bridge. I had hoped for a V2 on this train but at least it was steam.

method of crossing the Tay with a linking ferry service. It must have taken most of the day for prospective passengers to travel between Edinburgh and Dundee prior to both the Forth and Tay bridges being opened, as both Firths were crossed by ferries.

The opening of the Tay Bridge in 1878 should have seen the Tayport branch's demise, but the bridge's dramatic collapse the following year restored its importance. When the second Tay Bridge was opened in 1887 the line went into obscurity, eventually closing in 1956; sections of it have been converted to a Sustrans cycle path. Meanwhile Tayport was to benefit, in 1879, with a second connection off the ECML – this time from a junction just south of the Tay Bridge at Wormit, the 4¾-mile branch being served by trains over the Tay Bridge from Dundee. This latter branch was truncated at Newport-on-Tay, due to the opening of the Tay Road Bridge in 1966, the remaining stub being closed completely in May 1969.

The line that I was about to travel over, between Dundee and Perth, had a very chequered ownership history. Initially opened in 1847 by the Dundee & Perth Railway, this concern was swallowed up by the Scottish Central Railway in 1863, only to be engulfed by the mighty Caledonian Railway just two years later.

The 14.00 departure for Glasgow out of Dundee that day was worked by a somewhat lost-looking Carnforth-allocated Black 5 45390 – a locomotive that was to plague me over the next three years while regularly working the Belfast

Home-allocated Vulcan Foundry B1 61180 is held at signals at Dundee Tay Bridge – she became one of the final two B1s to be withdrawn in May 1967.

Deri Express, it would hold the audacity to work a leg of one of the many 'last day of steam' specials in August 1968. I caught this train in order to connect into another summer Saturday service, the 14.55 Perth–Edinburgh, which two weeks previously had been worked by a V2. What did I get? 2 D5306 (Class 26)! Over my lifetime I have amassed a library of books depicting steam scenes from those years and that very month Dundee's V2s, 60818 and 60973, were both photographed working summer Saturday services – no more need be said.

I nevertheless adhered to my plan and travelled south the 34½ miles to Inverkeithing. Opened in 1860, this line, which was not included in the Beeching recommendations, via Kinross Junction was controversially closed in 1970 to make way for the M90 Perth–Edinburgh motorway. This road was constructed along most of its course from Bridge of Earn to Cowdenbeath, resulting in trains between Perth and Edinburgh nowadays having to operate over the far lengthier route via Newburgh and Ladybank. This wonderfully scenic route, with a 6-mile climb up a 1 in 75 gradient from Bridge of Earn to the summit in the Ochils at Glenfarg, would have been much better appreciated had the power been steam rather than a DL. Alighting from this train at Inverkeithing (I hope you are following all this on the map!), a

A pair of J37s, 1921-built 64623 nearest the camera, at rest at Alloa shed on the evening of Saturday 24 August 1965. I had alighted here to travel over the doomed branch line to Larbert. It was to close in January 1968 as the repair costs of the swing bridge across the River Forth were not considered financially viable for the handful of trains per day that used it.

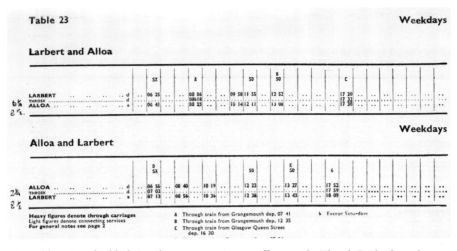

Timetable extract highlighting the sparse service on offer over the Throsk Bridge branch.

connecting DMU took me to Alloa in order to travel over the doomed Alloa–
Larbert branch.

At Alloa – a station that appeared to be in a time warp with many arte-
facts underscoring its North British Railway legacy adorning the station walls
– I was able to wander at will around the adjacent steam shed during the
25-minute connection time I had there. There were three 0-6-0s present: J38
65922 and J37s 64571 and 64623. Over the other side of the station, on the
Kinross Junction branch (closed in June 1964), DSLs D2716, D2744 and D3345
were berthed.

The 5½-mile Larbert–Alloa line started life in 1850 when a branch was
opened from Larbert to the south bank of the River Forth, opposite the harbour town of Alloa. Passengers and freight were taken across by ferry until 1885,
when a twenty-span, 1,615ft long swing bridge was opened; although the line
was not listed in Dr Beeching's report, the cost of maintaining the bridge for
the five daily passenger trains was no doubt the deciding factor in its demise.
Closure to passengers came in January 1968, and the swing bridge was fixed
open to shipping in May 1970; even though the bridge was demolished the
following year, the piers and abutments still stand to this day.

Arriving into Larbert at 18.09, there was just time to dash over the footbridge to catch another one of the ten consecutive-numbered St Rollox
Caprotti Standard 5MTs, 73153 (oddly embellished with a yellow smokebox
number plate), which was working that evening's 17.35 Glasgow–Dunblane
service. Taking this train just a few miles north to Stirling, I subsequently read
that it was delayed later into its journey at Gleneagles, behind the preceding

The 17.35 Glasgow Buchanan Street–Dunblane storms away from Stirling with
Riddles-designed 4-6-0 73153 – another one of St Rollox's stud of Caprotti Standard 5MTs.
Subsequently transferred to Stirling, albeit for storage purposes only, she was withdrawn in
December 1966.

Right time, right place! Usually a BR 5MT, the 18.15 Glasgow Buchanan Street–Dundee Tay
Bridge was that evening worked by one of the three remaining A2s – 60528 *Tudor Minstrel*.
Seen here at Perth, she was to be transferred from her then home shed of Dundee to Ferryhill
to cover for the ailing A4s, prior to withdrawal in June 1966.

'St Mungo' – that train's locomotive A4 60009 *Union of South Africa*'s tender overheated with hot bearings.

As stated in the preceding chapters, the three remaining Dundee-allocated A2s were sporadically reported as having stood in for failures over the summer. That evening's normally Standard 5MT-worked 18.15 Glasgow Buchanan Street–Dundee was gratifyingly powered by 60528 *Tudor Minstrel*. So I had an A2 instead of a V2 – I sat back, satisfaction overwhelming me, listening to her attacking the almost 3 miles of 1 in 88 paralleling the scenic Allan Water encountered after the Dunblane call. You never knew what surprises or disappointments you would encounter each time you set out – it was all par for the course back then; I wouldn't have changed it for the world! Ferryhill's A4 60019 *Bittern* could be seen at Perth shed when passing by that evening, she being, at the time, one of three remaining A4s I required for haulage.

So it was the end of another day's chasing around Scotland. Once again deliberately homing in on Perth for my bed home for the night (on the 20.25 London departure), I took the opportunity to purchase an evening paper, which had some football information from that day's matches; Scotland's top two teams had both suffered defeats, with Rangers going down to Aberdeen and Celtic to Dundee – both losing 0–2. Further south and Charlton Athletic's midfielder Keith Peacock made history by becoming the first ever substitute to be used in a Football League match, at home against Bolton Wanderers.

The 20.25 Perth–Marylebone departure was, that night, another mundane Black 5 – but from Carstairs the locomotive I viewed earlier that day at Carlisle, 72007 *Clan Mackintosh*, took me over Beattock. What a fitting finale to a perfect day. This train, taking the same route as two weeks previously, suffered a 51-minute late (09.11) arrival into Marylebone that Sunday morning. Overall, the 1,119-mile outing cost, because I veered off route from my BR pass, 5s 11d. Even though I rarely noted the weather, on this trip it appears I made an exception: it was raining on both overnight journeys but dry when it mattered during the day. With the cessation of a great many short-dated summer Saturday trains (indeed the 20.25 Perth–London ceased running altogether) the following week, I had no further plans to visit Scotland that year.

Will I reach Aberdeen by steam next year? Will I *ever* catch a run with a V2?

Looking through my collection of *Railway World* magazines while researching for this book, I realise now that I was extremely fortunate to achieve all that I managed during my visits to Scotland that year. The reign of the A4s on the Aberdeen–Glasgow services was becoming weaker by the autumn of 1965. Several NBL Type 2 diesel locomotives (Class 21) had been equipped

with Paxman engines and were introduced on the northbound 'Grampian'
and the southbound 'Granite City' by November. With further re-engined
examples (designated Class 29) becoming available the following month, some
of the Glasgow–Dundees were also dieselised, displacing the St Rollox Caprotti
Standards. The reliability of the diesels, however, often resulted in steam replacements, Ferryhill sending out borrowed Brits, Clans, Black 5s and A2s, as well
as an isolated use of V2 60818.

On the rail-tour front, the final remaining A3, 60052 *Prince Palatine*, although
having successfully worked a tour in early September, failed a boiler test just
prior to a December tour and was replaced by A2 60532 *Blue Peter*, herself failing at Carlisle, with Dundee's 60528 *Tudor Minstrel* being dispatched post-haste
to replace her. Sister 60530 *Sayajirao* was also in action working an Edinburgh–
Birmingham relief as far as Carlisle on 18 December. Staying on the Waverley
route, a month prior to that, on 18 November, BR 2MT 78049 (64G) worked
the 06.30 Hawick–Carlisle and 18.13 return – oh how I would liked to have
been aboard that!

Meanwhile the A4s began falling by the wayside, with 60026 *Miles Beevor*
being withdrawn in December and 60007 *Sir Nigel Gresley* placed in storage
pending preservation. Elsewhere the WR rid itself of all steam locomotives
(except a handful associated with the thwarted closure of the S&D) at the turn
of the year. Indeed, the statistics for the year highlighted the dramatic inexorable decline of the iron horse. BR started 1965 with 4,990 steam locomotives
on its books, after a decrease over the previous year of 2,054, but ended up
with a mere 3,003.

7

SCOTTISH VISITORS
DOWN SOUTH

INTO 1966 AND even though the BR deficit was growing ever faster, perhaps not helped by two 3½ per cent wage increases extracted by the railway unions, the government was investing millions of pounds in the railway system: modernising stations, electrification projects, colour light signalling, new depots, power signal boxes and bright new build diesel and electric locomotives adorned with BR's double arrow symbol. CWR (continuous welded rail) was being laid countrywide – a frustrating side effect being the inability to calculate speeds off rail joints in the darkness. Two of the largest closures, the S&D and the ex GCR, were enacted that year. Numbers of steam locomotives were falling month on month.

On to non-railway newsworthy events from the beginning of that year and the first credit card (Barclay's) made its appearance – not that I possessed one until many years later upon becoming a mortgage holder. The post-war affluence amongst those in work was now growing fast, with more and more families becoming car owners and motorways being constructed all over the country to cope. Then there was the premature death (aged 52) of broadcaster Richard Dimbleby at the end of 1965, pirate ship *Radio Caroline* running aground off the Essex coast in January, John Lennon's controversial statement that 'we are more popular than Jesus' causing uproar and, on the very day of the subject of this chapter, a mongrel dog called Pickles found the missing FIFA World Cup trophy in a South London garden.

With the price of beer going up, to 1s 10d, together with the hemline of miniskirts (both attractions being deferred for a couple more years!), my priorities in chasing the ever-dwindling numbers of steam locomotives throughout the country merely intensified.

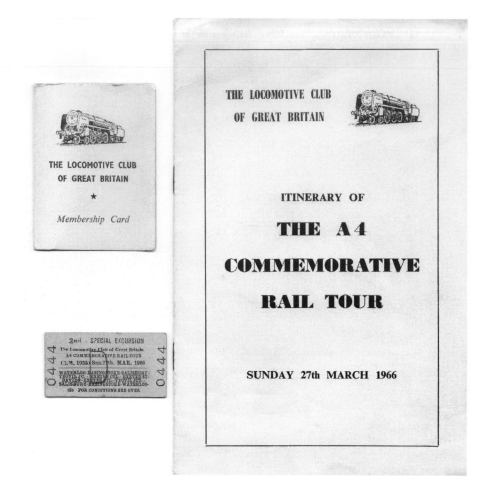

LCGB ephemera in connection with the A4 Commemorative Tour from Waterloo to Exeter and return on Sunday 27 March 1966.

I am unsure as to my reasoning behind travelling on the LCGB-organised A4 Commemorative Tour on Sunday 27 March, given that I had caught the selected locomotive, St Margarets-allocated A4 60024 *Kingfisher*, on her home country's territory the previous year. Perhaps I was hoping for one that I hadn't travelled with. Or perhaps it was the novelty factor of steam over a route that, following the 1963 regional boundary changes, had been awarded to the WR, over which, from September 1964, services had been monopolised by their Warship DLs. One of Nine Elms' more spirited drivers, Porter, was in charge for the first leg of the journey to Salisbury. He managed to coax, despite a great many speed restrictions en route along with several signal checks, a maximum of 84mph down the bank approaching Andover Junction. Putting in a fine performance as befitting their 'streak' nickname, several more speeds

A4 60024 *Kingfisher* calls for water replenishment at Salisbury en route west. This shot was the best obtainable due to the surrounding crowds!

Now at Exeter St Davids, soon after arrival *Kingfisher* is about to be detached and sent LE to Exmouth Junction for servicing and turning. A Hymeck DL was to assist her up the 1 in 36 incline to Exeter Central, after which several instances of 80mph plus were recorded over the then double-tracked former LSWR main line.

It was a normal Sunday activity for us haulage bashers, having arrived into Bournemouth on the 09.33 (excursion) train from Waterloo, to sleep or play footy on Bournemouth West Cliff. Curiosities aroused, having heard an unusual chime whistle from the direction of the Central station, some of us dashed there and found the now preserved A4 60007 *Sir Nigel Gresley* being serviced at 70F. The date was Sunday 3 June 1967 and the locomotive was on the second of the locomotive's two-day visit to the SR.

of 80mph plus were recorded along the then double-tracked ex LSWR main line to Exeter. With a similar scenario of high-speed running encountered on the return train over the same route, an almost on-time arrival at Waterloo of 19.37 completed a very pleasant 345-mile day's outing. *Kingfisher* returned safely to St Margarets before transferring to Ferryhill for her final months prior to withdrawal in September that year.

Back to Scottish railway matters and (for one month only!) the 08.25 Glasgow and 17.15 Aberdeen were diagrammed for Birmingham Type 2 (Class 26/7) DLs reverting to steam haulage in April, but with now only three A4s fit for purpose (60019, 24 and 34), Dundee's A2 60528 *Tudor Minstrel* was reallocated to Ferryhill to assist. On the WCML services, two trains, the 09.25 ex Crewe and 13.35 ex Euston, continued to be Kingmoor Brits resourced from Carlisle to Perth.

8

CARLISLE CALLING

CARLISLE, LOCATED AT the confluence of the rivers Eden, Caldew and Petteril, is the city and county town of Cumbria (née Cumberland) and is 10 miles south of the English–Scottish border – 299 rail miles from London Euston. Starting life as a Roman settlement established to serve forts on Hadrian's Wall, it became a military stronghold thanks to the many wars between England and Scotland. The imposing castle, which dominates the city, was constructed during the reign of William II (1087–1100), a period when Carlisle was wrestled from Scottish to English control. Indeed Carlisle exchanged ownership between the two countries on many occasions over the years – until the 1707 Act of Union settled the matter. The introduction of textile manufacturing due to the Industrial Revolution turned Carlisle into a densely populated mill town, thus attracting several railway companies vying to provide services.

Carlisle Citadel station was opened in 1847 in a neo-Tudor style to the designs of William Tite. It was then one of three stations in the city but by 1851 had become the main one. It was expanded and extended in 1875 upon the arrival of the Midland Railway. Most of the routes from the station remain in use, the only significant casualties being the former North British Railway line to Silloth (closed in September 1964) and Edinburgh via Hawick (the Waverley Line, closed in January 1969). The layout has also undergone few changes of any significance other than the singling of the ex NER Tyne Valley route down to London Road Junction as part of the 1972–73 re-signalling scheme associated with WCML electrification. There are eight platforms provided, three through and five bay, the substantial buildings on both the western island and the main

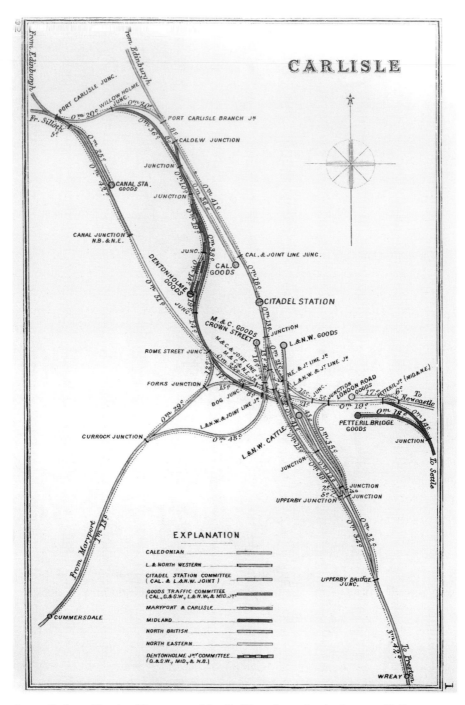

A 1912 Railway Clearing House map of the Carlisle and associated rail routes. (Railway Junction Diagram, Wikimedia Commons)

up platform on the east side being linked by a wide footbridge. Freight trains formerly used a goods line to the west to bypass the station, but this was closed in 1984 after a runaway rake of container wagons derailed at high speed on the River Caldew Bridge at Denton Holme, damaging the crossing beyond economic repair. Nearly all freight services (apart from those running directly between the Workington line toward either Petteril Bridge Junction or the Settle route) now have to use one of the main platform lines when passing through the station, which can cause congestion at peak times.

I first briefly called in at Carlisle's Citadel station in August 1964 while travelling between Newcastle and Preston, arriving on a DMU and going forward over Shap with Black 5MT 45209. During the following year, as have been detailed in previous chapters, the stopovers at Carlisle station were just that – merely setting foot on Carlisle's platforms to ascertain the number of the changeover locomotives taking me either onwards into Scotland or home-bound to London. The drawback of being a baby boomer was that by the time I became interested in steam all the Stanier and Fowler express class of steam locomotives, which prior to September 1964 had monopolised the major-ity of Class 1 expresses, had been dispatched to the breaker's yards; English Electric Type 4 (Class 40) and latterly Brush Type 4 (Class 47) diesels were now the dominant traction. Those services that remained steam operated, although monopolised by Britannia and Stanier 5MTs, did spawn the occasional surprise appearance of a Clan or Jubilee.

How many readers from that steam-orientated era remember the station's atmosphere you were able to drink in back then? The staff canteen, open 24/7, providing sustenance for weary enthusiasts (never challenged!) was conveni-ently located at the south end of the up platform – meals sometimes wolfed down if steam unexpectedly took over a train instead of the rostered DL. Some wag, no doubt a regular gricer, had chalked a wall adjacent to the entrance with 'due to increased patronage we are pleased to announce lower prices' – some hope! If funds were short, however, an alternative food source was the sixpenny chocolate machine on the up platform, which if hit in the right place provided a continuous supply! Then there was the forerunner of the Dymo tape: a huge red machine with an enormous pointer for selecting a character and a large handle for embossing it. Instead of tape, a thin aluminium foil was dispensed that came out in the shape of a totem – all for the price of a penny. This was often utilised not for its original purpose, to print your own name, but rather the names of steam locomotives recently caught. There was also the down-side waiting room with its continuously fed coal fire. Another activity, which I personally never witnessed elsewhere, was the wheel tapper as he made

This photograph of Stanier 4-6-0 North British-built Jubilee 45584 *North West Frontier* at Carlisle, having arrived with a local service from Scotland on Saturday 22 August 1964, perfectly portrays the station where I was to spend what amounted to four days of my life waiting for steam trains. The atmosphere, particularly at night with locomotives sitting in the middle road awaiting their trains, of smoke and safety valves lifting under the overall roof, will be forever etched upon my memory. The scourge of electrification paraphernalia had yet to ruin the scene, and the often-crossed footbridge still remains.

The south-end pilot at Carlisle the same day was LMS 3F 0-6-0T 47326. This Upperby-allocated 'Jinty' was transferred to Lostock Hall, being withdrawn there in December 1966.

his way along the trains while they changed locomotives – his responsibility, upon hearing a sound indicating a defect, was to order the errant vehicle to be taken out of service.

Carlisle, the entry point of all bar one of my steam incursions into Scotland, was statistically the third, after Preston and Wigan North Western, station where the greatest amount of my time was spent waiting for required haulages. During those hours spent there all train movements were monitored – constant reference to both timetables and STNs being made in case, as often occurred, a requirement necessitating travel on the train about to be worked by it was to be boarded. A 'requirement', to those readers unfamiliar with the term, is a locomotive that hadn't a red-lined entry in my Ian Allan *ABC*, which indicated a steed I had yet to be hauled by. Monitoring all departures, it wouldn't have been unusual for us (no, I wasn't alone in my quest) to be observed wandering nomadic like, usually at night, the length of this vast station. Trawling through my records (a pastime only possible having reached retirement), I have calculated that I spent four days of my life waiting (festering in modern jargon) for steam-worked passenger trains at Carlisle. Always seemingly busier during the night hours, Carlisle station was a veritable cathedral of steam. Attentive passengers straining to hear any announcements must have given up all hope when the locomotives' safety valves lifted, their firemen having to keep the locomotives in perpetual readiness under the cavernous roof. It mattered not in what direction they were to travel because, being a BR employee, free passes valid for all lines were kept to hand. Unlike today's scenario in which the internet and planned resourcing means a guaranteed locomotive, the lows and highs associated with anticipated catches often being thwarted or unexpected surprise appearances was par for the course back then.

Moving on to the motive-power scene, at the beginning of the 1960s, there were three sheds providing resources for services radiating out of Carlisle. Canal shed's allocation, predominantly comprising LNER classes including some A3s, were used on the Waverley, Settle and Newcastle roads. Whilst Upperby had the prestige Patriots and Princess Coronations for the WCML services, in contrast Kingmoor, the largest of the sheds, had an allocation in excess of 100 comprising a miscellany of types, the Stanier Black 5s being, as ever, the most dominant. The only 'namers' at 12A were a dozen or so Jubilees, a handful of Scots and Duchesses, and five Clans; except the twenty-two Crabs, all other representatives of classes, i.e. LMS tanks, 4Fs and 8Fs, were in single figures.

It was in May 1965 that I first briefly glimpsed Kingmoor shed in the early hours of a Saturday morning when passing by on my Stranraer-bound train.

The area it covered seemed vast, taking into consideration the majority of SR depots I was used to seeing being diminutive in comparison. Witnessing dozens of locomotives, their smoke drifting over the surrounding fields, was to me an awesome sight. The actual allocation was a sizeable 118. The order was, however, changing rapidly, the migration of Britannias from all over the country being the most pronounced. The 'namers' were now made up of sixteen Britannias, four Clans, two Royal Scots and a solitary Jubilee. BR Standard 9Fs (seventeen) were now the second most sizable type there, the balance being made up of Ivatt's Moguls and a few LMS tanks.

My first visit of any length, and indeed the only one on which I ventured further than the nearby chippy outside the Citadel station, was on Thursday 31 March 1966 and having arrived in Cumberland courtesy of the overnight Euston–Whitehaven sleepers (a service that was discontinued within weeks), I made my way to Carlisle over the soon to be closed scenic Lake District route via Cockermouth, and set off for Carlisle's Kingmoor shed.

The Ian Allan publication *British Locomotive Shed Directory*, compiled by Aidan L.F. Fuller, came into its own here. An essential guide for enthusiasts attempting to negotiate unfamiliar streets, I followed the instructions to the letter:

> Leave Carlisle station by the main entrance and go straight ahead into Court Square. Turn left along English Street and continue into Scotch Street and Rickergate. Cross Eden Bridge and continue up Stanwix Bank. Turn left at the top along Etterby Street and continue along Etterby Scaur. Turn left at the top of the hill into Etterby Road. A broad cinder path leads to the shed from the right hand side of this road (just before the railway bridge). Walking time 45 minutes.

I am certain that I have, over the years, avoided obesity due to the physical requirements and stamina necessary to follow my hobby!

It was the largest shed I would ever visit. It was of Caledonian Railway origin, which was bestowed with 12A as part of the London Midland Region when the coding system was introduced upon nationalisation. Then housing over 140 locomotives, it was only a short time later (May 1950) that it became aligned to the Scottish Region and was recoded 68A. The meddling, costly, bureaucratic authorities, so often prevalent within government-owned organisations, then resigned the shed back to the LMR in February 1958 – returning its code to 12A. And so it stayed until its closure to steam on 1 January 1968. The resultant effect on the former LNWR shed at the south of Carlisle, Upperby, was that it went from 12B to 12A to 12B on the similar dates, closing its doors to steam in December 1966. The third shed at Carlisle, the former North

Forty-eight years after first viewing her at the back of Kingmoor, Stanier 4-6-0 Royal Scot 46115 *Scots Guardsman* arrives into Wymondham station while participating at the Mid Norfolk Railway's 2014 Spring Gala with the ECS to form the 12.05 for Dereham. The sense of achievement at finally catching a run with her after all those years was surely a testament to the skills and dedication of a great many volunteers within the preservation movement. Thank you!

British Railways establishment of Canal, which veered from 12B to 68E to 12C on a similar timescale, closed its doors to steam in June 1963.

Unlike its sister shed at Upperby, visited 2 hours later, no photographs were taken; perhaps not being in possession of the legally required shed permit, I sneaked around trying to be as inconspicuous as possible. Taking into account it was a weekday when a lot of the residents were out and about, there were just thirty-one locomotives present. The most significant, from my point of view, was the sighting of a Scot on BR metals – 46115 *Scots Guardsman*, which had been withdrawn that January. She had been sporadically used through 1965 on Waverley-routed summer extras and, in September that year, on a Carlisle–Blackpool Illuminations special with the last reported working of taking the 09.25 ex Crewe forward to Perth on 31 December. To have witnessed her back then – looking forlorn in a siding at the back of the shed, chimney covered with sacking awaiting towing away to the breaker's yard – and to see the results of the preservation movement's hard labour as she now runs around the country is truly miraculous. Here are the details of those 'cops' (all home depot allocated unless otherwise shown):

In steam	43121, 44708 (67A), 44878, 44886, 44985 (5D), 44991 (66B), 45061, 45105, 45107 (10D), 45126, 45137 (8C), 45442, 45450 (10A), 47326, 47641, 70005 *John Milton*, 70008 *Black Prince*, 70016 *Ariel*, 70037 *Hereward-the-Wake*, 70046 *Anzac*, 73131 (9H), 92015, 92018(9D), 92051, 92114
Dead	44668, 45148*, 45530 *Sir Frank Ree**, 46115 *Scots Guardsman**, 73057 (67A*), 92009

★ Withdrawn

Then to the roundhouse-equipped Carlisle Upperby afterwards:

Leave Carlisle station by the main entrance and go straight ahead into Court Square. Turn right into Botchersgate and continue into London Road. Turn right into Tyne Street (just past the railway underbridge). This is a short cul-de-sac, and a cinder path leads to the shed from a gate at the end. Walking time 20 minutes.

On shed	41217, 41222, 41285, 44658 (8B), 45188 (8C), 45212 (12A), 45340, 45390 (10A), 46426, 46455, 46513, 70001 *Lord Hurcomb* (12A), 70010 *Owen Glendower* (12A), 70011 *Hotspur*, 70020 *Mercury*, 70022 *Tornado*, 70029 *Shooting Star*, 70030 *William Wordsworth*, 70032 *Tennyson*, 70048 *The Territorial Army 1908–1948*.
Withdrawn	44939, 70018 *Lightning*

This and the following six photographs were taken on Thursday 31 March 1966 when visiting 12B Carlisle Upperby shed. A representative of a class of locomotive I never personally saw out and about in the area, 'Mickey Mouse' Ivatt 2MT 41217, is resting between duties. She had had a varied nomadic life being allocated at several Manchester area sheds then Southport before arriving at 12B in February 1965. She was withdrawn upon the shed's closure to steam in December 1966.

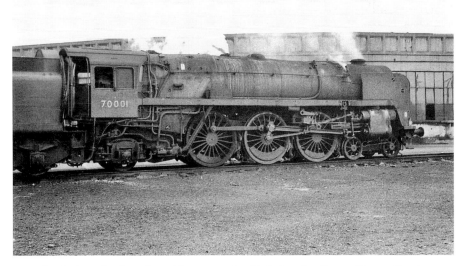

Upperby shed, on the day of my visit, was awash with Britannias. Former Eastern Region Brit 70001 *Lord Hurcomb*, named after the first chairman (1948–53) of the then newly created British Transport Commission, is seen here. Her days ended at the nearby Kingmoor depot just five months later.

Ivatt 2-6-0 46513, once a long-term Oswestry resident but displaced here in June 1965, awaits the call to duty. With little work remaining for a 2MT, she was dispatched to the cutter's torch four months hence.

Former WR-allocated, then Crewe North, Brit 70019 *Lightning*, with her coupling rods no doubt recycled to a more active sister, awaits her move to the scrap yard.

Another former Cardiff Canton resident Brit 70022 *Tornado* is seen at rest. One of the more active Brits at her new home of Kingmoor the following year, she was withdrawn in December 1967.

Former Longsight- and Willesden-allocated Brit 70032 whose *Tennyson* nameplates had become lost at rest in Upperby shed.

Sister Brit 70029 *Shooting Star*, also a prime performer on services out of London Paddington, is seen at rest at 12B. She was to take me over Shap at 3 a.m. six months later, prior to being reallocated to 12A.

9

THE QUINTINSHILL VISIT

MY FIRST VISIT of 1966 into Scotland was aboard the Fellsman Rail Tour of Saturday 4 June. This LCGB-organised tour departed Euston at a respectable time of 08.25, which, unusually during that year, gave me a bonus of a Friday night in the comfort of my own bed. A well-polished Stockport Edgeley Brit, 70004 *William Shakespeare*, took over at Liverpool Lime Street and was joined at Carnforth by the unique (she was equipped with outside Stephenson valve gear) Kingmoor-allocated Black 5 44767. Good timekeeping was adhered to over Shap and, having travelled through Carlisle station and via the then new marshalling yard opposite Kingmoor steam shed, the itinerary showed us as terminating at Gretna Junction. In fact we progressed over the border (thus qualifying a mention in this book!) a further 1½ miles to Quintinshill – scene of the infamous train crash in 1915 at which over 200 passengers perished. I had travelled on this tour principally for the Jubilee haulage and had anticipated, with both expected to be from LMR sheds, to collect runs with two required locomotives. Would you believe it, the *only* Jubilee I'd ever had a run with before, Leeds Holbeck's 45593 *Kolhapur*, was one of the two that returned the train south! At least the second Jubilee, Stockport's 45596 *Bahamas*, was required.

A mere 7 minutes later we set off south, taking the 'new' freight flyover into Kingmoor Yard then avoiding the Citadel station by taking the rarely used (by passenger services) goods lines to Petteril Bridge Junction. Travelling over the scenic Midland Railway route via Ais Gill before turning west over the then freight-only route via Whalley to Blackburn, Crewe was reached a mere 13 minutes late at 19.32. Then the fun started: due to overhead line problems along the Trent Valley we eventually departed 98 minutes late, Type 4

THE LOCOMOTIVE CLUB
OF GREAT BRITAIN

ITINERARY OF

THE

FELLSMAN

RAIL TOUR

SATURDAY 4th JUNE 1966

Front cover of the rail tour brochure for the Fellsman Rail Tour from London Euston to Quintinshill and return on Saturday 4 June 1966.

Qualifying for a mention within this Scottish-orientated book because of its penetration over the border to Quintinshill, the train is seen here (in extremely crowded conditions) at Liverpool Lime Street with Stockport's Brit 70004 *William Shakespeare*.

D302 hauling a dead E3174 via Bescot, relinquishing the train solely to the AC Electric loco at Rugby Midland. Congestion, regulation, whatever, we eventually limped into Euston 203 minutes late at 00.53. Back then there were

The reason for my participation on the Fellsman Rail Tour was the booked use of Stockport's locomotives, the depot, by then, not having any regular passenger work. Here the double-chimneyed Jubilee 45596 *Bahamas* is seen at the Blackburn water stop en route south.

no alternative arrangements, in the form of paid-for taxis or hotel rooms, for passengers to complete their journeys as there are for present-day travellers. The Underground had ceased running and, although there were hourly interstation buses, there was nothing like the night bus network London now has. I doubt if I ever considered taking a taxi – the end of the queue was out of sight anyway – so, with my knowledge of London's streets being far better than anywhere else, I started walking.

En route home you might think? I don't think so – the steam-worked 03.15 papers Waterloo–Southampton Terminus was unusually diverted, because of engineering work, via the normally EMU-only routes of the Guildford New Line and the Pompey Direct. Bulleid Light Pacific 34004 *Yeovil* was the power for that wonderful dawn-breaking summer morning ride and, having alighted at Eastleigh and now fully awake, I made the most of this unexpected visit to the area and headed for Woking on a Warship-hauled train in order to colour in 'the Alps' on my map, indicating which routes I had travelled over with steam, Bullied Light Pacific 34025 *Whimple* working that day's 09.33 (excursion) Waterloo–Bournemouth Central. Finally, with the line via Basingstoke now open, I slept back to London on a Merchant Navy 35030 *Elder Dempster Lines*-powered service, eventually arriving home 16 hours later than planned with an unexpectedly healthy 515½ steam miles in the bag!

10

BRIEF ENCOUNTERS

PERHAPS IT IS NOW opportune to summarise the Scottish steam scene. By May 1966 overall numbers had declined to just 323 steam locomotives resident on Scottish soil. Four sheds, 64C Dalry Road (Edinburgh), 65C Parkhead, 65F Bathgate and 64G Hawick, had closed and of the Pacifics all the A3s had disappeared and the A4s were down to five (albeit only three in service) and the V2s to seven. One of Bank Hall's remaining Jubilees, 45627 *Sierra Leone*, made two incursions into Scotland that spring, both on Liverpool–Glasgow 'footex' trains in connection with that year's European Cup Winners' Cup. First in April when Celtic beat Liverpool 1-0 and second the final in May when Borussia Dortmond beat Liverpool 2-1 at Hampden Park.

Excluding the three 24-hour sojourns undertaken, detailed in the following three chapters, to Scotland made during 1966, there were also two flying visits on Friday 1 July and Friday 19 August. They have been grouped together here because an almost exact schedule was adhered to. My normal work days were Monday to Friday so what was the attraction of taking a much-valued day's annual leave you may ask? The answer was the 13.27 (FO) Manchester Victoria–Edinburgh Waverley which only ran from 24 June to 2 September that year, on which you could obtain runs with six different steam locomotives en route (yes, bankers count!). This was because the main through locomotives worked from Liverpool Exchange to Carlisle and from Carlisle to Glasgow Central, the portions attached at Preston (from Manchester) and detached at Carstairs (for Edinburgh) providing a further two. On the main portion from Liverpool, the previous summer this train had several prestige locomotives working it, namely Bank Hall's Jubilees 45684 *Jutland* and 45721 *Impregnable*, as well as the final surviving Scot: Kingmoor-allocated 46115 *Scots Guardsman*. With the Liverpool shed allocation of Jubilees down to one, 45627 *Sierra Leone*, there was always hope – but, perhaps seeming a little ungrateful, I was only to get Brits and Black 5s.

I had departed Euston that July morning to the strains of The Beatles' 'Paperback Writer', their tenth number-one hit, being played over the tannoy. The 09.00 ex Euston was a complete set of blue and white coaches and a prize example of Britain's modern railway. Although, taking into account the rail industry was going through a step change into the future with modern, cleaner and faster trains in an attempt to encourage more custom, it meant by default the demise of the steam locomotive was drawing ever closer. I had mixed feelings on the matter, as although the steam locomotive was the focal point of my hobby, the railway industry was my career and had to modernise – or sink into oblivion against the inexorable tide of motorways being constructed.

Having walked across Manchester from Piccadilly to Victoria stations, a well-trodden path which would have been far easier if today's metro system had been in place, it was back to reality with a grimy, maroon, six-coach set that awaiting me for the 222-mile journey ahead. Departing bang on time, Newton Heath-allocated Black 5 45133 took us (my friend Bob and I) the 30¾ miles to Preston where she relinquished her train to Bank Hall's sister 44809 for the 90-mile trek over Shap. The by then eleven-coach train somehow lost 20 minutes en route to Tebay, further delay being accumulated awaiting the return of Tebay's Fairburn tank 42251 from banking a preceding freight. At Carlisle, where very few steam trains went through without an engine change, Kingmoor turned out Brit 70033 *Charles Dickens* for the border crossing, after which she accomplished the 40-mile journey to Beattock in 47 minutes, maxing at 68½mph along the only slight downhill section en route approaching Nethercleugh.

The Caledonian Railway had opened this route throughout in 1848 – accessing Glasgow – having agreed running rights over the Glasgow, Garnkirk & Coatbridge Railway into a terminus at Townhead. This unsuitably positioned terminus was quickly sidelined a year later when a slightly more direct line from Motherwell via Newton and Rutherglen into the Glasgow, Barrhead & Neilston Direct Railway's terminus at Southside was opened. It wasn't until some thirty years later that Glasgow Central station was utilised. Beattock itself was a mere hamlet – Moffat, the birthplace of Lord (Hugh) Dowding, architect of the Battle of Britain, 2 miles distant, was the nearest town of any size. It was to here, during Victorian times, that people suffering ill health travelled to in order to 'take the waters', believing that the high sulphuric mineral content was therapeutic for their ailments. A connecting branch line there was opened

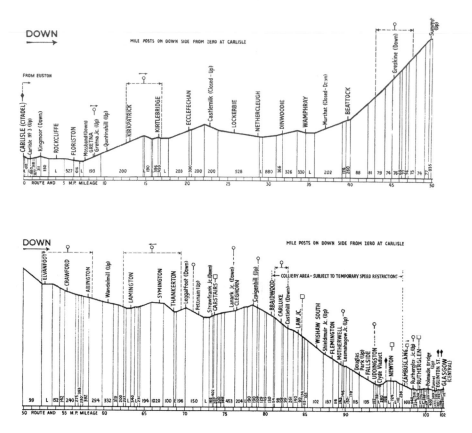

The gradient profile of the Caledonian main line over Beattock.

in 1883, but insufficient patronage caused passenger services to be withdrawn as early as 1954.

Beattock shed (66F) never possessed more than six locomotives, of either Fairburn or Standard tanks or 76xxx, during 1965–66 and, although lasting until April 1967, they were down to two during their final months. With Fairburn tank 42274 (on loan from Carstairs?) buffered up at the rear, the struggle started and it was, without doubt, necessary to 'window hang' in order to witness the sight and sound of the two steam locomotives hard at work. Immediately start-ing at 1 in 88, the gradient steepening in places to 1 in 69, the 10-mile battle to the 1,015ft-high summit was undertaken in just over 17 minutes, the speed falling from a steady 39mph to 28½mph when passing MP 49. If all that wasn't enough, the spectacular scenery of the forested slopes of the Southern Uplands, with its myriad streams and rivers, passing by surely fulfilled the utopian dream.

The Beattock summit sign. (© RuthAS and licensed for reuse under the Creative Commons Licence)

	Gradient	Time	Speed
Beattock station		00.00	
MP 41	1 in 88	03.20	34
MP 42	1 in 81	04.57	38½
MP 43	1 in 79	06.29	39
MP 44	1 in 79	08.00	39½
MP 45	1 in 74	09.33	39
Greskine	1 in 76	10.06	39
MP 46	1 in 69	11.04	38
MP 47	1 in 74	12.36	39
MP 48	1 in 75	14.12	36
MP 49	1 in 74	15.57	28½
Summit		17.19	31

This is what we lived for during those years: the sight and sound of man and machine battling against the gradient, creating a lump in the throat and tears to the eyes (the latter courtesy of the smuts and smoke) – a wonderful sense of

exhilaration to us steam followers! The fact that it was all disappearing made
you feel like you were witnessing history in passing.

With the summit breasted and now given an easy ride, *Charles Dickens*
accomplished the following 23½ miles down the other side to Carstairs in
even time, maxing at 78½mph through Lamington. It was here, in early 2016,
that Storm Frank demolished the railway viaduct spanning the River Clyde,
leading to a closure of over two months of the WCML. The Edinburgh portion
of three vehicles was detached at Carstairs, with St Margarets-allocated Black
5MT 45127 depositing us at Waverley station 51 minutes behind schedule at
19.41. What a wonderful 6 hours of steam travel – well worth taking one of
my annual leave days off for. Although the train also ran on Saturdays, the two
portions were often worked separately and, with smaller loading, didn't require
banking – and frequently worked by DLs to boot!

Always on the lookout in the relevant region's timetable for the wavy-lined
dated FO or SO services (they being the most likely to be steam powered),
Bob and I headed north on a DMU the 26 miles to Kirkcaldy. We had spotted
a 19.45 FO (24 June–26 August) Aberdeen–Edinburgh, which for three Fridays
only (1, 8 and 15 July) was extended to York. This suited us down to the ground,
as the following day we were to go Jubilee chasing in the Bradford area. At
Kirkcaldy – a town that elected Labour's Gordon Brown (Prime Minister of
the UK between 2007 and 2010) as its MP 2005–15 – we went on an eventually
successful search for a bite to eat. However, upon our return and witnessing the
pleasing sight from behind the ticket barrier of Ferryhill's Black 5MT 44703
arriving into the station, we were 'advised' that regulation tickets were necessary
to enable us to board. With the booking office being closed, the ticket barrier
staff were somewhat reluctant to let us through without the guard's acceptance
of a ticket irregularity. Completely unaware of this requirement, and concerned
that we could be stranded there for the night, upon production of our ever-
present BR identity cards (a regular ploy often successfully used to travel on
ECS or visit motive-power depots), we were ushered aboard the half-full train.
After steaming over the Forth Bridge, the lights of Edinburgh hove into view
and, with the Black 5 handing over her train to a Brush Type 4, we departed
just before midnight, stretching out in a compartment for some well-deserved
sleep, for York. It was just as well the train terminated there because it was
some time after the arrival time of 04.12 that we were shaken awake by the
station staff who wanted to send the train to the sidings without any passengers
aboard. We had headed for this area in order to catch runs with some of the
country's few remaining Jubilees and, having rubbed the sleep from our eyes, a
resplendent 45562 *Alberta* sat waiting for us on the 04.35 Leeds departure, the

tales of travels in that area having been published in my *Riding Yorkshire's Final Steam Trains* book of 2015.

Having blitzed the NER all day on Saturday 2nd, the following morning found me arriving into Euston at 06.20. Was I headed home? Not with the prospect of a run behind a class of locomotive that had escaped my clutches on several occasions last summer. The LCGB organisation had, after the success of their A4 tour on the Southern Region four months previously, decided to repeat the scenario – this time with a V2. How could I refuse a run with one so close to home? The locomotive earmarked for the tour was Dundee's 60919 but, having arrived several days earlier, failed just hours before the tour at Nine Elms with a broken spring. Unaware of this fact and having idled away a considerable amount of time in cafes and on station benches awaiting the departure of the Green Arrow tour out of Waterloo at 09.52, upon learning of its replacement power, namely Light Pacific 34002 *Salisbury*, I dejectedly decided, having been once more thwarted in my attempt to catch a run with this seemingly elusive class of locomotive, to cut my losses and go home. I subsequently read afterwards of the superhuman attempts to make the V2 fit to pick up the tour later in its itinerary. She was patched up and sent light engine to Eastleigh with the intention that she would take over the tour there. However, on arrival at Eastleigh, her injectors were proving temperamental and the control office at DMO Wimbledon decided wisely that it was a total liability and sent it back LE to Nine Elms – only for it to fail at Basingstoke with an overheated bearing. This, by default, gave the tour's participants a fleeting glimpse of it at the Basingstoke shed. To rub salt into the wound, after her return to Scotland she worked Dundee–Glasgow services on four occasions that month – needless to say I wasn't around!

So, now to my second flying visit to Scotland that summer. Seven weeks later, on Friday 19 August, the exact same schedule was replicated – unfortunately with a 33 per cent reduction in steam catches. In the news the previous day was the opening of the Tay Road Bridge – one of the longest (just short of 1½ miles) road bridges in Europe. It replaced 'the Fifie' ferry service across the River Tay to Newport-on-Tay and also was complicit in the closure of the railway branch line there. More recently a competition, ran by a local radio station, to find a slogan for the bridge, which has gradual slope towards Dundee, had to be abandoned; 'it's all downhill to Dundee' was deemed inappropriate. Musically The Beatles were back at the top of the charts, this time with their double-sided 'Yellow Submarine'/'Eleanor Rigby'.

Once again I had taken a day's leave, but this time I had started out the previous evening and spent the early hours of that Friday festering, along with some of society's ne'er do wells, at the minor four-star-rated Preston waiting room pending the start-up of train services. Presenting myself at Manchester Victoria for the 13.27 departure, Newton Heath had turned out her Black 5 44818 on this occasion. Stockport-allocated sister 44868 took the eleven-vehicle train forward from Preston and, after having made an unscheduled stop for water at Carnforth, took her train unaided over Shap, breasting the summit at 15mph. With no Brit available at Kingmoor, the foreman sent out home-allocated Black 5MT 44989. At least a banker was provided at Beattock, albeit a Standard tank that I'd had a run with a year previous when allocated to Hurlford – 80111. To cap it all a 'Sputterbug', or as younger Scottish enthusiasts have nicknamed them 'Mac-rats' (alluding to the fact that they had seemingly overrun train services north of the border), Type 2 D5066 (Class 24) took over the Edinburgh portion at Carstairs. So six became four!

Trekking, as before, north to Kirkcaldy for the 21.45 ex Aberdeen, pleasingly worked by Perth's 44997 – a locomotive destined to become 63A's sole allocation the following April – I didn't note any problems boarding on this occasion. Back at Edinburgh the schedule varied from before and, by catching the 23.55 departure for Birmingham, a train that was booked for steam haulage south of Carlisle, the Carstairs avoiding line was travelled over. This service, other than on summer Fridays, would normally have been a portion for Carstairs, joining there with a similarly formed portion from Glasgow, but between June and September they ran as separate complete trains.

II

GRANITE CITY BOUND

AS READERS MAY recall from earlier chapters detailing my exploits during the summer of 1965, I made several attempts to reach Aberdeen by steam that year, the late running of the Anglo-Scottish overnights always thwarting me. Also I had yet to obtain a run behind those seemingly elusive Gresley V2s (now down to eight in number); often they were reported as operating services I was not aboard. Well here we go again! By the summer of 1966 there were just nine remaining Jubilees within the NER and one of the trains they were booked to work was the 21.20 FO (1 July–26 August) St Pancras–Glasgow Central between Leeds City and Carlisle.

Setting forth on the evening of Friday 8 July, to the strains of The Kinks' 'Sunny Afternoon' which was topping the charts, out of London, I arrived into Leeds City during the early hours of Saturday, and the now familiar sight of Jubilee 45593 *Kolhapur* backed on to take me the 113 miles over the Pennines to Carlisle. Usually booked to change locomotives at Carlisle with a DL working forward, on this morning, duly replenished with more water, she continued the 116 miles via the ex G&SWR route via Dumfries and Kilmarnock to Glasgow Central. There were quite a few enthusiasts aboard all of whom, myself included, had planned to alight at Carlisle and await the commencement of the daytime WCML summer-dated services – predominantly Brit hauled – some hours later. It was about 5 a.m. and, with nothing else liable to happen during those early hours, a great many of us returned to our seats if only for the novelty of a Jubilee run into Scotland.

Back in those frenetic days anything unexpected such as the aforementioned meant an ad hoc revision to any planned itinerary and, having rejoined the

The front cover of the 1966
Scottish Region Timetable.

Although having noted several of her sisters in Scotland, this is my only photograph of one
of the twenty-strong BR 3MT class. Built in 1954 and initially spending her formative years
on NER metals, this ex Northwich transferee 77014 is seen at her new home of Guildford in
November 1966.

Glasgow train, immediately began studying the ever-present Scottish timetable accordingly. This service called at Kilmarnock en route and I had to make a decision upon reaching there as to whether to continue forward to Glasgow or alight for an Ayr-bound train. Why was the decision so hard? It was either a high-mileage attempt at reaching Aberdeen by steam or a ride with Hurlford's 77007 on the 07.15 departure for Ayr. By taking the local to Ayr, the next nearest anticipated steam journey would probably have meant returning to Carlisle, wasting several valuable hours in doing so, and so I forfeited the one and only chance of a ride with one of these 77xxxs in normal service − forever. The only one I caught was the sole transferee into the SR of 77014 on a rail tour over the Windsor branch.

So, after a 10½-hour journey travelling in LMS short wheel base carriages, I arrived, for the very first time, into Glasgow's largest terminus − Central station. It was indeed an impressive sight. Opened in 1879 by the Caledonian Railway, it was provided with eight platforms linked to the former terminus of Bridge Street on the south bank of the Clyde by a four-tracked bridge. Extra tracks were added in 1905 and the station expanded to thirteen platforms to cope with increased patronage. The station's famous architectural features are the large glass-walled bridge that takes the station building over Argyle Street, nicknamed the 'Hielanman's Umbrella' by locals because it was used as a weatherproof gathering place for visiting Highlanders, the former ticket office, platform, and the train-destination information building. This was an oval building, with the booking office on the ground floor and the train information display for passengers on large printed cloth destination boards placed behind windows on the first floor by a team of two men; these were replaced in the 1980s by a new travel centre. Underneath the 'Umbrella' is a bustling array of shops and bars, as well as the Arches nightclub, theatre, gallery and restaurant complex. During the early 1960s overhead power lines had been installed in connection with Glasgow Electric train services − followed, in the 1970s, by the WCML electrification itself. Further expansion is proposed in connection with the controversial much-delayed Glasgow Airport rail link.

Back to 1966 and, having arrived 30 minutes late, at 08.00, into Glasgow Central, there was still ample time to walk across to Buchanan Street for the 08.25 'Grampian' departure for Aberdeen. Unbeknown to me at the time, a mere three A4s remained in active service for the 3-hour expresses, the shortfall of A4s being covered by a mix of DLs, Black 5s and an A2 (*Blue Peter* was transferred to Ferryhill from Dundee to replace withdrawn *Tudor Minstrel*). Although I was fortunate that morning, with 60024 *Kingfisher* performing the haulage honours, I silently cursed at having caught her before in Scotland as

Scottish Steam's Final Fling

Top extract (1965)

48720 6200F | 48961 5399?

10720 14F		61035 * 50A	61275 50A	62006 52D	63405 52G	64580 65F	65842 52F
48729 2F	60124 * 51A	61040 * 56A	61278 62B	62007 52G	63406 52G	64588 62A	65844 50A
48730 10D	60129 * 50A	61042 40E	61281 62B	62008 51A	63407 51C	64595 62A	65846 50A
48731 9F	60145 * 50A	61049 50A	61285 40E	62010 50A	63409 52A	64597 62B	65851 52F
48735 8E	60151 * 50A	61050 41J	61289 50B	62011 52D	63410 52C	64599 62C	65853 52G
48736 5B	60528 * 62B	61051 41J	61293 62B	62012 50A	63413 51C	64602 62B	65855 52F
48738 5D	60530 * 62B	61055 36A	61302 40E	62017 NER	63417 55H	64606 62A	65859 51A
48739 10A	60532 * 62B	61058 40B	61303 50A	62021 52D	63420 55H	64608 62B	65860 52F
48740 9K	60806 51A	61072 62C	61304 56B	62022 52D	63421 51C	64610 65F	65861 52F
48741 9E	60810 50A	61087 36A	61306 50B	62023 52D	63426 55H	64611 62C	65862 52F
48742 8A	60813 64A	61089 40E	61307 64C	62024 52F	63429 52F	64618 62A	65865 52G
48743 9J	60816 64A	61092 40E	61308 64C	62025 52D	63431 52H	64620 62B	65869 52F
48744 9D	60818 62B	61099 64A	61309 56F	62026 52G	63435 51C	64623 62C	65872 52G
48745 9H	60824 64A	61101 62C	61313 41J	62027 52F	63436 52G	64624 62B	65873 52G
48746 8A	60831 50A	61102 62B	61315 41J	62028 50A	63437 52G	64632 62A	65874 52F
48747 2F	60835 64A	61103 62A	61319 50A	62041 51A	63440 51C		65879 52F
48748 9L	60836 62B	61110 56B	61322 56B	62042 50A	63443 51C		65880 52F
48749 6B	60837 50A	61115 56F	61324 64A	62044 51A	63445 52G		65882 52F
48750 16G	60844 62B	61116 65A	61326 36A	62045 51A	63446 51C		65885 52G
48751 5E	60846 64A	61121 36A	61329 36A	62046 50A	63450 51C		65892 52F
48752 2F	60868 52A	61123 56A	61330 62A	62048 51A	63453 52H	65234 64A	65893 52F
48753 5E	60876 50A	61131 56A	61337 50A	62050 52D	63454 51C	65243 * 64F	65894 50A
48754 6B	60877 50A	61132 62A	61340 62B	62057 50A	63455 52H	65267 64F	65901 62A
48755 2E	60886 50A	61133 62A	61342 65A	62059 51A	63458 52G	65282 64F	65903 62C
48756 9D	60919 64A	61134 64C	61343 62A	62060 50A	63459 52F	65288 62C	65905 62A
48757 2C	60940 52A	61140 65A	61344 64A	62062 50A	63612 41J	65297 64F	65907 62A
48758 9D	60946 52A	61145 40E	61345 64A	62065 50A	63639 40E	65319 62B	65909 62A
48759 15A	60952 52A	61147 62B	61347 64C	62067 NER	63644 40E	65327 62A	65910 62A
48760 82F	60955 64A	61148 62A	61348 36C		63653 36A	65345 62A	65911 62A
48762 2E	60970 64A	61158 36A	61349 64A		63674 40E	65788 52G	65912 62C
48763 16G	60973 62B	61161 56A	61350 64A		63675 40E	65789 52F	65914 62A
48764 8F	60976 52A	61172 62B	61354 64A		63730 36A	65790 52F	65915 62A
48765 9D		61173 56A	61360 36A		63764 36A	65795 52F	65916 62A
48766 2F		61176 50A	61361 40E		63770 40E	65796 52F	65917 62C
48767 2F		61180 62B	61384 40B		63781 40E	65801 52F	65918 62C
48768 5D		61188 40E	61385 56B		63785 36A	65802 52F	65920 62A
48770 9H		61189 * 56F	61386 56F	63344 55H	63788 36A	65804 52F	65921 62C
48771 10D	61002 * 50B	61195 36C	61387 56A	63346 52G	63816 40E	65805 52F	65922 62A
48773 9K	61003 * 40E	61199 50A	61388 56B	63347 51C	63818 36A	65809 52F	65925 62C
48775 9D	61008 * 65A	61210 40E	61389 36C	63349 51C	63819 40E	65811 52F	65929 62C
	61010 * 50B	61216 50A	61390 40E	63360 52H	63843 41J	65812 52F	65931 62C
	61012 * 50B	61223 40B	61394 41J	63362 52F	63858 40E	65813 52F	65932 62A
	61013 * 56B	61224 56A	61403 62B	63363 52H	63873 40E	65814 52F	65934 62C
	61014 * 56F	61232 56F	61404 64A	63366 52H		65815 52F	
	61016 * 56F	61237 * 56B	61406 40B	63367 52H		65817 52G	
60004 * 61B	61017 * 56B	61238 * 56B	61407 62C	63371 52H		65819 52F	
60007 * 61B	61018 * 50A	61240 * 56B		63377 52H		65821 52F	
60009 * 61B	61019 * 50A	61244 * 64A		63379 52H		65823 50A	
60019 * 61B	61021 * 50A	61248 * 40E		63381 52F		65825 52F	
60024 * 64A	61022 * 56A	61250 * 40B		63384 52H		65831 52G	
60026 * 61B	61023 * 56F	61255 50B		63386 52F	64547 62B	65832 52G	68006 9L
60031 * 65B	61024 * 56A	61256 50A	62001 51A	63387 55H	64569 62A	65833 52G	68012 9L
60034 * 61B	61026 * 40E	61261 62A	62002 52F	63389 52H	64570 62A	65834 52F	68079 9L
60041 * 64A	61029 * 64A	61262 62B	62004 51C	63394 51C	64571 62A	65835 52G	
60052 * 64A	61030 * 56B	61263 62B	62005 50A	63395 52G	64576 62B	65838 52F	
	61032 * 50B	61264 40E		63397 51C	64577 62B		
				63398 52H			

16 | 17

Bottom extract (1966)

48547-62067 | 63344-73127

48547 9K	48685 16B	48765 9B	61240 * 56A		65795 52F	70002 * 12A
48548 5D	48687 16B	48766 5D	61255 50B		65804 52F	70003 * 12A
48549 9B	48690 16B	48767 5D	61262 62C		65811 52F	70004 * 9B
48550 10F	48692 8C	48768 5D	61263 62B		65812 52F	70005 * 12A
48551 5B	48693 8E	48770 9H	61278 62B		65813 52F	70007 * 12A
48552 9L	48695 9F	48773 9K	61289 50B		65815 52F	70008 * 12A
48553 9H	48696 16B	48775 9H	61303 50A	63344 52H	65817 52F	70009 * 12A
48556 2E	48697 6A		61306 50B	63346 52G	65823 52F	70010 * 12A
48557 9D	48699 9F		61307 64A	63366 52H	65833 52G	70011 * 12B
48559 9D	48700 9H		61308 62A	63368 51C	65834 52F	70012 * 12A
48600 16B	48701 9F		61309 56F	63377 52H	65835 52G	70013 * 12B
48602 9D	48702 9K		61319 50A	63381 52H	65838 52F	70014 * 12A
48603 2E	48703 55B	60530 * 62B	61330 62A	63387 52H	65853 52G	70015 * 9B
48604 16B	48705 2B	60532 * 62B	61337 50A	63394 51C	65855 52F	70016 * 12A
48609 16B	48707 10D	60813 62B	61340 62C	63395 52G	65860 52F	70018 * 12B
48612 9F	48708 9F	60824 64A	61342 65A	63397 51C	65865 52G	70020 * 12B
48613 9F	48709 8C	60831 50A	61347 62A	63405 52G	65869 52F	70021 * 9B
48614 8G	48710 55D	60836 62B	61350 62C	63407 51C	65872 52G	70022 * 12B
48617 16B	48711 8C	60868 64A	61354 62A	63413 52H	65879 52F	70023 * 12A
48618 10D	48712 10A	60955 64A	61386 52F	63419 40E	65880 52F	70024 * 12B
48620 16B	48714 9H	60976 64A	61388 56F	63426 52H	65882 52F	70025 * 12A
48622 55B	48715 8F		61407 62A	63429 52H	65885 52G	70026 * 9B
48626 9B	48717 8E			63431 52H	65892 52F	70027 * 12A
48631 8E	48720 9F			63436 52H	65894 52G	70028 * 12A
48632 6A	48721 55D			63437 52G	65901 62A	70029 * 12B
48636 9H	48722 8G			63440 51C	65903 62C	70031 * 12B
48637 10D	48723 6A			63450 51C	65909 62A	70032 * 12B
48639 8E	48724 2B	61002 * 50B	62001 51C	63455 52H	65911 62A	70033 * 12A
48640 8E	48725 2E	61008 * 66E	62004 51C	63458 52H	65912 62A	70034 * 12A
48641 55B	48727 8G	61012 * 50B	62005 52F		65914 62A	70035 * 12A
48643 8E	48728 16B	61013 * 56A	62007 52H		65915 62A	70038 * 12A
48645 16B	48729 2E	61014 * 52F	62008 51C		65917 62C	70039 * 12A
48646 2E	48730 10D	61017 * 50A	62011 52F		65918 62A	70040 * 12A
48648 8C	48731 9F	61019 * 50A	62012 50A	64547 62B	65920 62A	70041 * 12A
48650 8L	48735 8E	61021 * 56A	62017 52F	64569 62A	65921 62A	70042 * 12A
48651 16B	48738 5D	61029 * 62A	62023 52H	64570 62A	65922 62A	70045 * 12A
48652 9K	48739 10D	61030 * 56A	62024 52F	64576 62B	65925 62A	70046 * 12A
48655 6A	48740 9K	61032 * 50A	62025 52G	64611 62C	65929 62C	70047 * 12A
48662 16B	48741 9E	61035 * 50A	62026 52H	64618 62A	65934 62C	70048 * 12B
48663 9H	48742 9D	61072 62C	62028 50A	64620 62C		70049 * 12B
48664 55C	48743 8A	61101 62C	62041 51C	64623 62C		70051 * 12A
48665 6C	48744 9L	61102 62B	62045 51C			70052 * 12A
48666 10D	48745 9B	61115 56F	62046 50A			70053 * 12A
48668 10F	48746 8A	61123 56A	62048 51C			70054 * 12A
48669 2A	48749 9H	61131 56A	62050 52G			
48671 9H	48750 8G	61140 65A	62057 52F	65234 64A		
48672 16B	48751 9B	61161 56A	62060 52F	65267 64F		
48673 16E	48752 2B	61173 56A	62062 52F	65288 62C		
48674 2B	48753 9L	61180 62C	62065 50A	65319 64A	68006 9L	73000 9H
48675 8F	48754 6A	61189 * 56F	62067 52F	65345 64F	68012 9L	73002 70G
48676 8L	48756 9D	61199 56A		65789 52F		73004 9H
48677 9F	48757 10F	61216 50A				73006 9H
48678 16B	48758 9D	61237 * 56A				73010 9H
48681 8E	48763 16B	61238 * 50A				73011 9H
48683 8E	48764 8F					
48684 9F						

(right-most 73xxx column:)

73014 9K | 73016 70G | 73018 70G | 73019 9K | 73020 70G | 73022 70A | 73025 9H | 73026 9K | 73028 9K | 73029 70A | 73033 9H | 73034 9H | 73035 9H | 73037 70A | 73038 6D | 73039 9H | 73040 9K | 73043 70A | 73045 9H | 73048 9K | 73050 9H | 73053 9H | 73059 66A | 73060 66A | 73064 66A | 73065 70A | 73066 9K | 73067 9K | 73069 9K | 73070 9K | 73071 9H | 73072 66A | 73073 9H | 73075 67A | 73080 * 70G | 73083 * 70G | 73085 * 70C | 73092 70C | 73093 70C | 73094 9H | 73096 9H | 73097 9H | 73099 66A | 73100 67A | 73102 67A | 73108 66E | 73110 * 70C | 73113 * 70G | 73115 * 70C | 73117 * 70C | 73118 * 70C | 73119 * 70D | 73120 67A | 73125 9H | 73126 9H | 73127 9H

12 | 13

Extracts from the Ian Allan *Locoshed* books of 1965 (top) and 1966 (bottom). Note the reductions, including the disappearance of all A4, A1 and A3s.

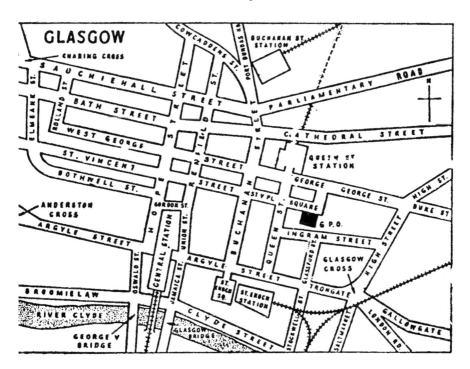

Glasgow street map extract out of Aidan Fuller's *British Locomotive Shed Directory*; note there were four railway termini back then!

One of the final three A4s in circulation, Ferryhill's 60024 *Kingfisher*, departs Stirling with the 08.25 'Grampian' Glasgow Buchanan Street–Aberdeen on Saturday 9 July 1966; she was withdrawn two months later.

EDINBURGH – INVERKEITHING – PERTH

Sc 21

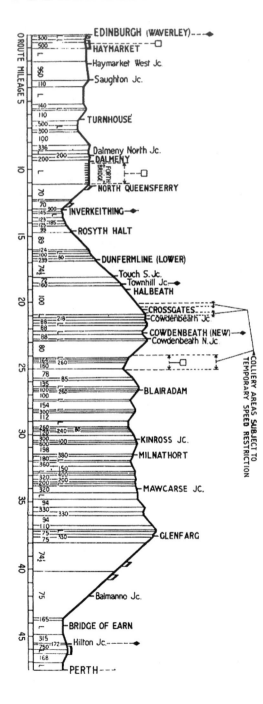

well as on a rail tour to Exeter that March – how ungrateful was that? To rub salt into the wound, the required 60019 *Bittern* had worked this service, I read in *The Railway World* magazine some months later, for six consecutive weeks at the beginning of the summer timetable. Taking into consideration that the objective of reaching Aberdeen with steam was missed out on several occasions last year, here I was possibly about to achieve my objective, and what did I do? Alight at Stirling!

In retrospect, looking at the moves I made during the next few hours, I have concluded that, at the time, I had prioritised a run with a V2 over reaching Aberdeen, as being of greater significance. To this end I travelled across from Stirling via Alloa to Dunfermline Lower to connect into a summer Saturday train that ran on only nine occasions that year, this being its second. The train concerned was the 10.45 Edinburgh Waverley–Inverness which I had heard, through the grapevine, was steam worked (no Type 4 DL available perhaps) the previous week due to increased loadings in connection with the

The gradient profile of the Glenfarg route.

Edinburgh Trades Festival – a V2 to boot! While waiting at Dunfermline Lower, the 10.30 Edinburgh–Aberdeen, another short-dated summer-only working, came powering through with Ferryhill's Black 5 44703 at its head. Had I missed yet another opportunity to reach Aberdeen with steam? My train duly arrived and, although it would have been churlish (surely!) of me to expect one of Gresley's 2-6-2s at least it was steam with St Margarets 45168 in charge.

It was a glorious sunny morning and 45168 had her work cut out in immediately having to climb for over a mile up the 1 in 74 incline to Crossgates prior to calling at Cowdenbeath. Then, seemingly riding over a raised plateau with the sun glinting off Loch Leven's still waters at Kinross and the heather-bound moors of Glenfarg, a wonderfully scenic 25-mile ride was enjoyed. As detailed in Chapter 6, when travelling the route on a DL-powered train, no more can rail travellers enjoy this panorama as the entire section closed in 1970 to construct the M90. Shortly after arriving into Perth, 63A's 45472 arrived with the Glasgow portion, the complete train being taken forward the 118 miles via Pitlochry and Aviemore to Inverness behind diesel power.

There was not long to wait for our (I was travelling with fellow enthusiast George who, even though he lived in Scotland, I had met on many occasions throughout Britain, chasing steam being the common dominator) next steam service in the form of Standard 5MT 73149 – my fourth St Rollox-allocated Caprotti catch. She was working the 11.00 SO (25 June–13 August only) Glasgow–Aberdeen as far as Dundee and, the rumour treadmill having gone into overdrive, was booked to be taken forward by Dundee's V2 60813. Although disappointed when 19-year-old B1 61263 was placed on the front, at least I was going to finally reach Aberdeen with steam. The 2-hour journey, in a Gresley-compartmented coach, alongside the visually scenic North Sea coastline, was thoroughly enjoyable. The 54½ miles north of Arbroath were until that day just destinations on a timetable, on a railway route I had long aspired to travel over.

Approaching Montrose, we travelled over a magnificent viaduct, to the west of which is a tidal basin, which crosses the South Esk River. Following the Tay Bridge disaster of 1879, this bridge, having been found to become distorted when trains traversed it when load tested, was rebuilt because of its similar design; the line eventually opened to passengers in 1883. The town, from which the eastern ridge of the Grampian Mountains can be seen, has vastly benefitted from trade in connection with the North Sea oil field and was another location only known to me beforehand as being an entry on the pools coupon – their football team languishing, at the end of the previous season, in the middle of the Second Division. Shortly after departing, Montrose Kinnaber Junction was passed; the signalman's decision at this location, where the nineteenth-century 'race to the north' trains operated between rival railway companies met, was often the deciding factor as to who would be the winner. Before reaching Aberdeen we called at Stonehaven. In recent times tourists from around the world have flocked to Carron's Fish Bar there to be photographed under the banner outside of the shop claiming 'birthplace of the world famous deep fried Mars bar'. The local council, however, have recently (2015) expressed their reservations about the situation, saying it gave the wrong idea about healthy eating.

Aberdeen, Scotland's third most populous city, is known worldwide as the Granite City, alluding to the fact that the majority of buildings, being constructed during the Victorian era, incorporated locally quarried grey granite. Since the 1970s, following the discovery of the North Sea oilfield, the city is more often referred to as the oil capital of Europe. The station currently standing was built as Aberdeen Joint station between 1913 and 1916, replacing an 1867 structure of the same name, on the same site. The station and the new Denburn Valley Line enabled the main line from the south, together with the commuter line from Deeside, to connect with the line from the north; the former had previously terminated at the adjacent Aberdeen Guild Street. Prior to the construction of the Joint station, lines from the north had terminated at Aberdeen Waterloo – a short but inconvenient distance along the edge of the harbour. This location, together with Guild Street, both became goods only after the construction of the Joint station.

As a result of the grouping of railway companies under the Railways Act of 1921, Aberdeen was shared by the LNER and LMS companies, each running the station for a year and then handing its administration to the other. Over the years following nationalisation, in an attempt to reduce costs, BR gradually withdrew services and closed lines in the surrounding areas. In the late 2000s the railway station was comprehensively refurbished. The original sandstone station building has become the centrepiece of a covered plaza for a new shopping and entertainment complex, while a granite-faced building was constructed to house station offices, a new travel centre and other facilities.

Aberdeen's Ferryhill shed (61B), passed just prior to arrival into Aberdeen station, had become, since the early 1960s, renowned for its allocation of A4s during their Indian summer, having seven out of the ten remaining Pacifics on its books. Numbers, however, were gradually reducing, with Dundee having to forfeit its A2s to supplant them on the 3-hour Glasgow expresses. The only other locomotives allocated there were, at the time of my visit, two Black 5s, two Standard 5MTs and three WDs. Of the three surviving A2s, the two I required, 60530 *Sayajirao* and 60532 *Blue Peter*, had both been accounted

B1 61263 at Dundee shed, taken on Sunday 16 October 1966. She was the very locomotive that three months earlier had taken me down the ECML to Aberdeen; her withdrawal came on the last day of that year. (Keith Lawrence)

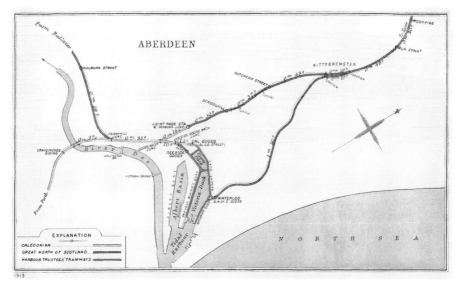

A 1913 Railway Clearing House map of Aberdeen's railways. (Railway Junction Diagram, Wikimedia Commons)

for that day — the first in light steam at Dundee shed and the second on the 13.30 'Grampian' from Aberdeen to Glasgow. Fingers having been crossed that *Kingfisher* would return to Glasgow on the evening 'Granite City', the 17.15 Aberdeen–Glasgow, became uncrossed as she backed down on to the six-vehicle formation just after 5 p.m. Further 'new' track awaited me along the Forfar cut-off – and what a run it was: mile after mile of high-speed steam the like of which I had only experienced in short stretches over SR metals. Gresley's streamlined Pacifics certainly saw their final days out in style.

Location	Miles	Time	Speed		Location	Miles	Time	Speed
Aberdeen		00.00			Glasterlaw		32.22	68
Ferryhill Jn		02.47	26		Guthrie		36.00	69
Portlethen		13.13	65		Clocksbriggs		38.17	70
Muchalls		15.06	77		Forfar	41½	40.55	
Stonehaven	16	20.30			Kirriemuir Jn		04.36	64½
New Mill Sdgs		08.30	60		Glamis		07.00	75
Drumlithe		10.09	70		Eassie		08.43	79½
Fordoun		13.24	75½/77½		Alyth Jn	12	11.45	82½/85½
Laurencekirk	14½	16.00	74		Ardler		13.26	85
Marykirk		18.38	75		Coupar Angus	17¾	15.06	85½
Craigo		20.17	78½		Burrelton		16.49	83½
Kinnaber Jn		22.10	75/40(pws)		Cargill		18.32	81
Dubton Jn		23.40	43		Stanley Jn		21.44	75½
Bridge of Dun	26	26.17	65		Strathord		24.07	72/sigs
Farnell Road		29.05	66½		Perth	32½	29.19	

The route taken by my train that day had been opened in the mid 1840s in piecemeal fashion, on each side of Forfar, by two separate companies. With certain sections being constructed to the Scotch gauge of 4ft 6in, the line was closed for conversion to the standard gauge in 1847, reopening throughout, by the Scottish Midland Junction Railway, in 1848. It was absorbed into the mighty Caledonian in 1866.

With the majority of the 'Forfar cut-off' running on lengthy levels, it attracted enthusiasts, looking to record high speeds, from all over Britain when the A4s were introduced on the 3-hour Aberdeen–Glasgow expresses in 1962. I was indeed fortunate because by the end of that month all three remaining A4s were out of service and, having spasmodically worked trains during that August, the ScR authorities organised a special the following month heralding the end

Notebook extract of that visit.

of their reign. The line over which I travelled that day, between Kinnaber and Stanley Junctions also was nearing the end of its existence, with closure coming in September 1967 after which all trains were rerouted via Dundee.

It would have been so easy to alight at Perth and catch the 20.25 homebound train for Marylebone, but alas it was missing from this year's timetable. Not being the heaviest loaded of services, passenger wise, I presume economics saw to its withdrawal. So what was the alternative route home? Always on the lookout to catch steam-hauled services wherever possible, I had espied the fact that 'The Northern Irishman' (22.10 Stranraer Harbour–Euston) was now, following the closure of the Port Road in 1965, rerouted via Ayr. To access that train I retraced the Glasgow cross-city walk undertaken earlier that day, crossing from Buchanan Street to Central station in order to catch the 21.00

DMU Stranraer departure, with the intention of alighting one stop short of its destination – Girvan. The best made of plans were always subject to 'right time' running and on this night, having suffered a 34-minute late start out of Glasgow Central because of mechanical problems, the train lost a further 21 minutes en route, finally struggling into Ayr at 23.00. I didn't risk going further south and alighted at Ayr, forfeiting a run with the recently transferred to Ayr, from St Rollox, Caprotti 73145 – the pilot assistance over the gradient-strewn section out of Stranraer to the main train locomotive Brit 70017 *Arrow*. Cross-checking with the Scottish timetable while compiling this book, I noticed that 'The Northern Irishman' called at Girvan 'for passengers destined for Carlisle and South thereof on request made to the Station master before 21.30 on the day of travel'. Although Girvan was a crossing point on the single line, *Arrow's* crew might have only exchanged tokens and not picked up any unexpected passengers – leaving me stranded for the night!

The loss of a run with the Standard didn't, however, detract from what I considered a very satisfactory visit. Thoroughly content with what I had achieved during that visit, off came the shoes and, after stretching out in an empty compartment, I was lulled to sleep listening to the exertions of my twentieth Britannia as she made her way, initially north, via Annbank, before joining the G&SWR line at Mauchline en route south. Late arrival into Euston on the Sunday morning at 09.05 (85 minutes late) was attributed, according to announcements, to a locomotive failure on a previous service. At 1,192 miles, it was my highest mileage weekend trip to Scotland to date and, although I had finally steamed into Aberdeen, I still hadn't caught a run with one of those elusive V2s!

12

CAUGHT AT LAST

EVERY WEEKEND DURING that summer of 1966 I was to be seen roaming Britain, homing in on train services shown within the various regional timetables embellished with a wavy line down the centre of the column. This indicated that it did not run for the entire validity of the publication it was contained in, the consequence being a greater likelihood of it being steam worked. Having blitzed the NER in an eventual successful mission to catch runs with the remaining North Eastern Region Jubilees, I was all set on Saturday 30 July, the day etched within English football history when they beat West Germany in the World Cup, to resume my chase after the Scottish V2s. I was, however, thwarted once again by the late running of the overnight Anglo-Scottish trains. I was on board the 21.20 St Pancras to Glasgow, which, because a drunken ATC had put his arm through a carriage window, was severely delayed at Sheffield. The incident required police attendance and detachment of the vehicle concerned, which inconveniently happened to be in the middle of the train. Although a stoic performance from Jubilee 45697 *Achilles*, which had taken over at Leeds, was made over the Pennines, the train was 95 minutes late running at Carlisle, where I decided to bale out. Had I have stayed aboard the train, with an estimated arrival time into Glasgow of 09.00, I would have missed the 'Grampian' departure out of Glasgow Buchanan Street as well as many connecting services over to the ECML.

There is a saying, 'if at first you don't succeed try, try again' – and so, two weeks later, on Friday 12 August, yet another attempt was made to locate a V2-hauled train. With two of Dundee's allocation, 60818 and 60919 (the errant V2 from the LCGB rail tour fiasco five weeks previous), having been reported on passenger services north of Edinburgh that month, *surely* my time had come.

Carlisle station, on the morning of Saturday 30 July 1966, was awash with Brits. Here, 70041 *Sir John Moore* waits to take over a Scottish-bound service. Returning south that morning with Brit 31 on the 07.50 departure, I never did catch a run with *Sir John*!

This photograph, together with the previous one, were, for whatever reason, never printed at the time and as such I have no record as to which trains they worked over the border that morning. 70032 *Tennyson*, which towards the end carried an improvised *Lord Tennyson* nameplate, readies herself for departure.

That year's footballing headlines had just about died down – being replaced by PM Harold Wilson's subsequently abortive attempt to kick-start the peace process over the Vietnam War with the Russians, and by an apology from John Lennon in regard to his 'Jesus' remark. Musically The Troggs were holding the top spot with their 'With a Girl Like You'.

I was with my friend Alan that trip and he, having obtained a LMR STN, had spotted a 21.50 (relief) Euston–Glasgow. Joy of joys with over 240 miles of Britannia haulage was savoured – 70010 *Owen Glendower* being exchanged with sister 70006 *Robert Burns* at Carlisle. Although unassisted over Shap, 66F turned out their Standard 4MT 76098 for Beattock bank, eventually depositing us at Glasgow Central 1¼ hours late at 07.50. The 08.25 'Grampian' out of Buchanan Street was a DL that morning and so we caught the 09.08 DMU departure via Falkirk and the Forth Bridge to Inverkeithing, on the off chance of there being, you've guessed it, any V2s in circulation. Just arriving in time for the 09.10 Dundee–Blackpool, a train that ceased to run the following week, what was working it that morning as far as Edinburgh? Only Dundee's V2 60813! Had 'The Grampian' been steam earlier that morning we would have caught it to Stirling, changing there and arriving on to the ECML after this train had headed south. The sense of achievement was euphoric.

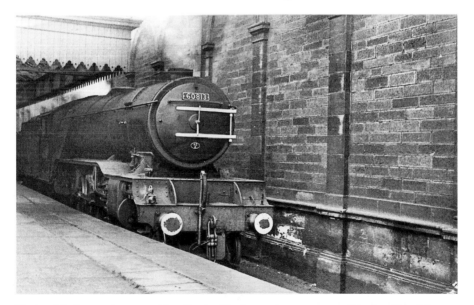

Having failed to catch a run with a Gresley V2 the previous year, one of the handful of the remaining examples, Dundee's 60813, is seen here at Edinburgh Waverley on Saturday 13 August 1966. This 29-year-old Darlington-built 2-6-2 had just brought me over the Forth Bridge whilst working that day's 09.10 Dundee Tay Bridge–Blackpool North. Hours of waiting and expectation over several trips to Scotland had finally resulted in this capture.

Edinburgh Waverley again and just 16 minutes later one of Carstairs' (66E) two Standard BR 5MTs, 10-year-old Riddles-designed 4-6-0 73108, readies herself for departure with the 11.25 portion to Carstairs. There it would be attached to the rear of a Glasgow–Manchester and Liverpool service.

My quest had finally been completed. All those miles and hours over the previous visits – for this! It was only 24 minutes. It was only 13¼ miles. With a mere nine remaining countrywide, one of which was at York, only a like-minded haulage basher can appreciate the amount of satisfaction I felt. 60813, which had been on the receiving end of attention by members of the infamous MNA organisation, was unique in being the only member of the class equipped with a short stovepipe chimney and small wing smoke deflectors. After having crossed the Forth Bridge prior to attaining a maximum of 67½mph through Turnhouse that day, she was condemned forty-four days later.

Mission accomplished, so to speak, and on a high, we decided that it would be more rewarding (because of the greater likelihood of steam-hauled trains) to head south and concentrate on WCML services in the Preston area. Not that we went there straight away. Compared with the syncopated three-cylinder exhaust beat of the V2, the 11.25 Edinburgh Waverley–Carstairs had an extremely vociferous Standard 5MT, 73108, at its head. What a run! Having stormed up Cobbinshaw bank, she then attained a glorious 81mph maximum on the downhill section between Auchengray and Carnwath. This six-vehicle portion was destined for Manchester and, while being placed on the rear of the

The summer Saturday 13.25 Glasgow Central–Morecambe Promenade, seen just prior to departure with a brace of Black 5MTs, was a regular double-headed working, the lengthy train being routed over G&SWR metals. Hurlford-allocated 45490 was subsequently transferred to Motherwell, where she was withdrawn that December, whilst 10A's 45227 fared slightly better, going on to Lostock Hall and not ending her days until January 1968.

DL-hauled main section from Glasgow, on which we had intended to travel on, a steam-hauled train drew in on the opposite side of Carstairs island platform. A quick reference to the timetable revealed that it was the 08.20 from Morecambe to Glasgow Central – another train ceasing to run after the following week – and so, with Carnforth's Black 5 45445 perhaps having worked through, we arrived into Glasgow Central for the second time that day behind steam.

It was now 1 p.m. and this was where we chasers just went wherever steam was going. With nothing planned, we espied two Black 5s brewing up in Glasgow Central's easternmost platform. It didn't matter where they were going: we going to travel on it. Alan and I dashed round to the train, only then ascertaining its destination. It turned out to be the 13.25 opposite-way working to Morecambe but unlike the inwards was routed via the G&SWR route – and was also finishing the following week. Oh how these short-dated summer Saturday trains, anathema to Dr Beeching who highlighted the wasted non-use of stock lying idle during the weekdays, were a blessing to a steam crank. So a mere 25 minutes later we were crossing the River Clyde for the third time that day with steam: Hurlford's Black 5 45490 assisted Carnforth's sister 45227 the 116½ miles to Carlisle. Recent research uncovered the fact that this very train was often Jubilee hauled, the locomotive off the 07.30 Glasgow arrival ex St Pancras being returned south. Three weeks later while working the diagram, however, *Hardy* disgraced herself by running short of coal at Kilmarnock and was assisted forward by Hurlford's 3MT 77019.

Returning to my travels, by changing trains at Carlisle on to the following 14.00 Glasgow–Manchester, we headed over Shap en route to the Preston area thoroughly satisfied with what Scotland had had to offer that day.

On the football scene, there were over nineteen matches played on that opening day of the Scottish football season – perhaps the most notable being a local derby between Dundee United and Dundee, which ended 2-0 to the former.

Was that the end of haulage by Scottish-allocated steam that weekend? Three Standard 5MTs, one Fairburn tank and one Black 5MT runs later saw us – sleep deprived – boarding the southbound 'Royal Highlander' when calling at Wigan North Western at 04.03 – 70 minutes late! We understood that this was due to a disruption to all Anglo-Scottish services that night from a landslip at Sanquhar – but more delay was to befall the train. Waking from a deep sleep at Rugby, information filtered through that we had had a 1½-hour signal stand at Stafford because an engineer's train had become derailed. On top of this, a second derailment, near Watford Tunnel on the previous day, had blocked three out of the four lines, leading to a further 30-minute delay. All this amounted to a 09.28 arrival (188 minutes late) into Euston. Why am I relating all this in a book about Scottish steam? We had just 24 minutes to make the 09.52 *Blue Peter* rail tour out of Waterloo!

We were young and fit back then and, by always keeping pre-purchased valid Underground tickets on us – thus avoiding ticket office queues (no Oyster-operated automatic barriers back then) – we just made it, by 3 minutes! The other contributing factor, which aided our dash across London, was that having undertaken many similar journeys over the past few years we knew the exact position within each train to place ourselves when alighting, at the very point of exit on to either another Underground line or main-line terminal.

The LCGB organisation, not having been dissuaded by the experience with the V2 the previous month, had organised a third attempt to run another Scottish locomotive on SR and WR metals. On Sunday 14 August one of Dundee's two remaining A2s, 60532 *Blue Peter*, was sent south to work the A2 Commemorative Rail Tour from Waterloo to Exeter and return. She, however, wasn't very well and, after having sat on Honiton bank (a cylinder cock was subsequently found to have jammed open) for a while, we eventually limped into Exeter Central 104 minutes late (15.14). Departing at 16.42 (162 minutes

Notebook extract of the 72-hour marathon.

Having missed Dundee's A2 60532 *Blue Peter* on several occasions when she worked passenger services in Scotland, it was perhaps ironic that I eventually caught her on my home region's territory of the SR. This Doncaster-built 18-year-old Peppercorn-designed A2 was caught on camera at Salisbury while working the A2 Commemorative Rail Tour on Sunday 14 August 1966.

late), after considerable efforts were made to rebuild her fire, she did indeed recover a few minutes up the GWML to Westbury. However, a decision was made upon arrival there, where she handed over to Brit 70004 *William Shakespeare*, to allow the Brit to work through to London, thus eliminating the 90-minute layover at Salisbury where *Blue Peter* was booked to reclaim her train. This move, together with Nine Elms driver Male achieving an exhilarating run involving several speeds in the mid 80s mph, ensured an arrival time into Waterloo of 21.25 – a mere 80 minutes down. The grand mileage total for that weekend's trip was 1,247¼, out of which a whopping 74 per cent (920½ miles) were steam – wonderful, unrepeatable days.

13

THE AYRSHIRE ATTACK

IN AN AUGUST 1966 press release, the Scottish Region had stated it was their intention to eradicate their steam locomotive allocation during 1967. Not having, as yet, bashed the Glasgow suburban services, I reasoned that a visit by myself was long overdue. At least, having looked back through my notebooks while compiling this tome, I believe that to be the premise for the trip. As for non-railway news, that September The Small Faces had ousted The Beatles' double-sided 'Yellow Submarine'/'Eleanor Rigby' off the number-one spot with their 'All Or Nothing' hit and Ronald 'Buster' Edwards had been arrested in connection with the 1963 Great Train Robbery.

So it was on Thursday 15 September that I once again selected the ever-reliable, for steam forward from Carlisle, 'The Northern Irishman' departure out of Euston as being my entry into Scotland. Benefitting from the full implementation of the WCML electrification, the departure time had moved back from 19.30 to 20.40, thus giving me a chance to call in at home for a change of clothes and some food. As there were now only eight remaining Brits I required for haulage, to say I was well pleased upon seeing 70009 *Alfred the Great* backing down for the 02.22 departure out of Carlisle would be an understatement. The journey to Stranraer, however, was not as visually gratifying as the one made sixteen months previously, the dawn on that September morning not breaking until our arrival into Stranraer at just after 6 a.m. Whichever route trains to Stranraer took (readers may recall the route was now via Mauchline and Ayr), there were hills to climb and assistance was deemed necessary from Ayr. Home-allocated Black 5 45423 was provided to overcome nearly 8 miles of 1 in 67 from Pinwherry through Barrhill to MP 16½. The wonderful sounds

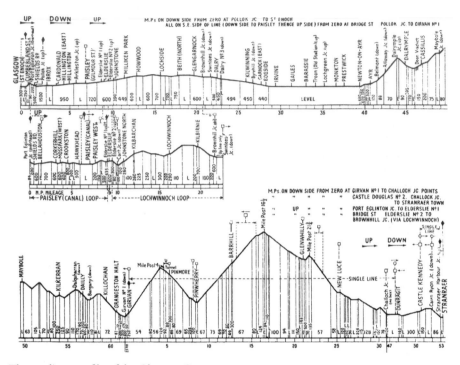

The gradient profile of the Glasgow–Stranraer route.

of the two locomotives vociferously struggling with their heavy train, and the reflections from their fireboxes dancing off the exhaust smoke being sent high in the darkness without doubt compensated for the absence of scenic viewing opportunities. With the train now traversing an extra 43 miles via its 'new' route, there was a side benefit of not having so long to wait – a mere 68 minutes – for the first train away from Stranraer back to civilization.

It would have been sensible to head straight to Glasgow if it was the suburban services I was after but I can only assume that by alighting at Ayr off the 07.35 DMU from Stranraer that I had hoped the Kilmarnock trains were still steam operated – by the 77xxxs? Looking through the timetables all these years later I can see that the train I caught, the 09.50 Ayr–Kilmarnock, had, along with many others along the branch, a figure 2 in a black bell symbol, indicating second-class only accommodation was available. Others, running at rush-hour times, didn't and I now realise those with the symbol indicated DMUs and those without were loco hauled, probably with steam! The steam locomotives' impending demise in the area became impossible to ignore when passing Ayr shed, which had numerous Hughes Crab 2-6-0s on the condemned line. At Kilmarnock I caught the 09.00 Carlisle–Glasgow that ran via Dalry and Paisley – a line that had lost its intermediate stations that April and was to completely close in 1973.

So there I was at Glasgow Central, ready to catch any steam suburban passenger services along the Gourock and Wemyss Bay lines, but they had all, certainly when off peak, gone DMU! Having expected at least the odd train to be steam powered, I had no alternative plans. I reasoned that perhaps the evening rush-hour extras might turn up trumps, but that was a long wait. A little after noon I noted a rake of non-corridor stock (research for this book revealed only a mere five sets were extant at the time of my travels) being propelled into the station by Corkerhill's Standard 5MT 73079. In a similar scenario as described in the previous chapter, having seen people board it, I dashed over and embarked myself – I was going to go wherever it took me! Upon conversing with other passengers, it turned out to be a 12.18 Race Special bound for Ayr in connection with a meeting being held that afternoon. That'll do for me! So 1½ hours and 40 steam miles later saw me alighting at Ayr noting some rather inebriated football supporters in the station refreshment room, presumably celebrating their local team's success at holding Scottish giants Rangers to

An unexpected catch was Corkerhill's Standard 5MT 73079 on a 12.18 Race Special Glasgow Central–Ayr, seen here after arrival on Friday 16 September 1966. She was to become one of the final thirty and was later withdrawn in May 1967.

The north end station pilot at Carlisle on 16 September was Ivatt Mogul 43121 – a locomotive that had spent the first decade years of her life at Cricklewood. With more water ending up on the platform than where it should have gone, she was one of the two Flying Pigs I was to catch on a Keswick branch 'Nunex' the following July, as well as on a rail tour over the border in November 1967.

At the south end on the same day was another former 14A resident, Horwich-built sister 43120 performing similar duties – she being the other Mogul caught into Keswick. She was less fortunate than her sister, being withdrawn three months earlier than her in August 1967.

Notebook extract.

a 1-1 draw in the Scottish League Cup quarter final first leg that week. Sadly, for them, their heroes were to lose 0-3 to them a week later in the second leg. Retracing my steps to Glasgow Central, and having hung around for an hour, there was still no sign of steam-worked suburban services and so I gave up the ghost, catching a Peak DL-operated (Class 45) train via the G&SWR route to Carlisle for that evening's 20.25 departure. One of my less successful Scottish steam-searching visits!

Scotland's home allocation of steam locomotives was now rapidly dwindling in number and by the autumn of 1966 the Scottish Region management suddenly woke up to the fact that there could be some money to be made by running some 'last of class' specials. First up were the A4s, a special being run on 3 September using 60019 *Bittern* on a Glasgow-Aberdeen and return train.

The last V2 excursion, featuring the sole surviving member 60836, is seen at Aberdeen on Saturday 5 November 1966. Withdrawn the following month, she was 'awarded' the demeaning task of heating passenger vehicles at Craigentinny (Edinburgh) Carriage Sidings for a few months into 1967. (Keith Lawrence)

She was also used that same weekend, together with sister *Kingfisher*, A2 *Blue Peter* and V2 60836, on a London-orientated 'Granite City' rail tour. Although rail-tour organisers often advertised certain locomotives they had on their trains as being the very last usage of them, it was often the case that they were subsequently sent out by the shed foreman on an ad hoc basis, substituting for a DL failure. This was the case for *Kingfisher*: she was dispatched on the 13th to work the southbound 'Granite City' and the following day to work the northbound 'Grampian'.

On 8 October it was time to say goodbye to the A2s. An Edinburgh–Carlisle and return was organised with 60532 *Blue Peter*, which, having been transferred to Ferryhill, was used, in a similar scenario to the A4s, on regular passenger trains as a substitute for a DL that failed on 16 and 17 November between Aberdeen and Edinburgh. The following month, having been booked for a special out of Edinburgh, she failed a boiler exam at St Margarets and was withdrawn.

Then it was the turn of the V2s: a commemorative tour utilising 60836 on an Edinburgh–Aberdeen special in the first week of November. Ferryhill turned her out again a week later for the southbound 'Bon Accord'. Also once more in action days later was *Bittern*, on a RCTS circular tour from York via Carlisle and Edinburgh.

Moving on to scheduled timetable services in early November saw a spate of 'last' or 'final' workings. On the 5th the 23.40 portion from Edinburgh Waverley to Carstairs was powered by Black 5MTs 45319 and 45129 – the final steam departure out of Edinburgh. That same day saw the final steam departure out of Glasgow Buchanan Street with B1 61330 on the 18.42 for Dunfermline. With Buchanan Street station itself closing on the 7th, the Dundee foreman attempted on two occasions the following week (B1 61278 and V2 60836) to dispatch steam on the now diverted services into Queen Street. The ban on steam down the bank into Queen Street was, however, upheld; the locomotives on both occasions were removed at Cowlairs. The G&SWR route also saw some surprise DL replacements that month, both on the 16.05 Glasgow Central–Leeds – Brit 70005 and Standard 5MT 73100 being the reprobates. Another occasional usage of steam replacement on the 19.44 Waverley-routed Carlisle–Edinburgh train was also reported. And finally, perhaps pre-empting the demise of the B1s, Dundee's 61278 was turned out for a last B1 circular tour from Edinburgh via Carlisle and Glasgow in December. The shed closures were now gathering momentum, with Eastfield, St Rollox and Dumfries closing in November and Bathgate, Greenock, Carstairs, Stirling, Hurlford, Ayr and Stranraer in December.

14

THE EVENING CARLISLE–PERTH

WHILE APPRECIATING THAT the previous chapter had taken us to the end of 1966, can I beg the reader's forbearance in briefly returning to the summer of that year to recall the two occasions I travelled on a train that was to enter Scottish railway folklore – the 20.25 Carlisle–Perth?

Trawling through the timetables of those years in connection with this book, I discovered that until the 18 April 1966 timetable change, a 13.35 Euston–Perth called at Carlisle from 19.54 to 20.27 and was presumably the forerunner of the train. This ceased to run through from London as a result of the revised timetable in connection with the WCML electrification implementation south of Crewe.

It was Saturday 6 August 1966 and, with The Beatles having released the album *Revolver* the previous day, steam services over the WCML were in full swing. Brit 70013 *Oliver Cromwell* was working that day's 13.20 Euston–Glasgow from Crewe and, aided by a signal stop in Preston platforms, a fair number of enthusiasts arrived into Carlisle at 18.40 that evening. As she was replaced by a DL, in true gricer fashion we wandered around the station aimlessly in the hope of something steamy turning up. Although it was a steep learning curve as to which trains were steam hauled and which weren't, at the tender age of 19 I was often found in the company of older and wiser enthusiasts. They didn't seem to mind us youngsters tagging along and some of them grouped around a telephone box on the platform while I hovered, curiosity aroused, nearby. Having studied both the STN and public timetables, I couldn't see the likelihood of steam going anywhere out of Carlisle within the next few hours and was on the point of returning south to Preston. The call being made was

PENRITH	u	13 47																			
CARLISLE	a	14 42		15 12		15 37		16 27		16 56 18 52 20 10				20 46		
	d	14 47		15 18		15 42		16 35		17 03 19 03 20 14		20 25		20 53		
HAWICK	a			17r59		16 59		19 43		19 45						
GALASHIELS	a			18r34		17 34				21 28						
DUMFRIES	a	17 23		17 23		17 23		17 23								
KILMARNOCK	a	18 29		18 29		18 29		18 29								
AYR	a	19 12		19 12		19 12		19 12								
STRANRAER HARBOUR	a															
PAISLEY GILMOUR STREET	a															
LOCKERBIE	a							17 34				20 57		
BEATTOCK	a							17 49				21 16		
CARSTAIRS	a			16 43 16 43				17 20	17 20	18 09 18 09 18 38		21 37 21 37 22 00		
	d			16 52 16 55						18 15 18 16		21 42 21 45 22 33 22 30		
HAYMARKET	a			17 27 17 47						18r46		22r17	23 08		
EDINBURGH	a			17 31 17 51						18 50		22 21 23 03 23 12		
MOTHERWELL	a			17 14				18 37		18 56	22 00	22 54		
GLASGOW CENTRAL	a	16 40		17 35				19 00		19 20 21 00 22 20		23q38	22 45	
OBAN	a	22x15		22x15							05x15	05x15	05x15	
COATBRIDGE CENTRAL	a									19 22		23 08		
LARBERT	a									19 39		23 31		
STIRLING	a									19 51		23 46		
PERTH	a									20 35		00 29		04 33
DUNDEE	a									21 38				07 11
FORFAR	a											01 35		08 06
ABERDEEN	a											03 20		07 53
INVERNESS	a											05 25		08 15

An extract from the 1966 timetable detailing the schedule for the 20.25 Carlisle–Perth.

to the Kingmoor foreman and the resultant news was that Brit 70006 *Robert Burns* was being turned out for the 20.25 Perth departure. In my naivety I was completely unaware that such a train even existed, let alone it being steam hauled, and, having been fortunate enough that day to have had a run of nine required locomotives (four of which were Brits), how could I refuse my fifth?

Those of us not requiring a run with *Robert Burns* returned south, leaving a party of just five whom, after having visited a chippy close to the station, returned in good time for the 20.25 departure. Resulting from late-running services from the south, it eventually left at 20.56. This featherweight train of two coaches and one van (indeed the smallest vehicle train booked for Brit haulage I was to come across) was, over the following eight months, to give me some sprightly runs over the 73 miles of ex Caledonian main line to Carstairs. The first few miles, part of which traverses along an embankment formed of deep moss which when being constructed absorbed thousands of tons of earth before becoming sufficiently stable, are through low-lying levels, the River Esk being the dominant waters, which in more recent times has seen extensive flooding. Taking full advantage of this, *Robert Burns*, although often checked by signals from the preceding train, achieved maximums of 70mph by Floriston, 76mph approaching Beattock, before topping the summit, having called at the station, at 48mph. We were able to sight the mileposts, thus enabling us to calculate speeds, due to the lengthy daylight hours Scotland is renowned for each summer. With the summit surmounted, a delightful late summer evening descent through the Vale of Annandale, the source of the Clyde, Tweed and Annan rivers, against a backdrop of the Greskin Hills was enjoyed.

The late start hadn't unduly concerned us because the timings column of this train indicated that a 33-minute station stop at Carstairs (to allow the

10.05 Euston–Glasgow, non-stop from Carlisle to pass) was scheduled. That night, with the station dwell time at Carstairs reduced to just enough time for all necessary duties to be carried out, we were a mere 3 minutes late into Coatbridge at 23.13 – the furthest north you could go without being stranded on a Sunday, taking into account the sparsely served Scottish railway system. We had just 30 minutes there before the only train returning us south, 'The Royal Highlander', was due and after being regaled as to who won the 'Big Fight' in London that day between Cassius Clay and Brian London (London got knocked out in the third round) by the porter there was just enough time to locate a local fish bar. We could never be certain, resulting from the haphazard nature of our hobby, when we would next have the opportunity to eat and so another portion of chips was consumed – the owner more used to home-going hungry drinkers at that time of night than an invasion of travel-stained 'anoraks'!

It was occasions such as this, when purchasing wares within Scotland, that I deliberately (out of pure devilment?) proffered my £5 or £10 notes, receiving as change several of the £1 notes issued by the seven Scottish banks. Over the following days in the south of England, I took a perverse delight in offering them to shopkeepers or publicans and witnessing the 'they aren't legal tender/oh yes they are' resulting dialogues – all but a minority eventually, usually after calling their managers, accepting them!

The returning 'Highlander' was very crowded that night and we had to stand or sit in the corridor for the 2-hour journey to Carlisle. As it was the last train of the overnight flight of services to London, we were resigned to suffering an uncomfortable journey home. Fortunately one of us had spotted in the LMR STN notice that the following Glasgow and Edinburgh to Birmingham train was shown to run as two separate portions and, as always with relief services, there was a chance of steam haulage south from Carlisle. This move paid off handsomely and, after supping some tea in the ever-open staff canteen listening to Brit 70002 *Geoffrey Chaucer*, our train locomotive, blowing off impatiently, upon its arrival we all headed for several empty compartments, took off our shoes and put our heads down, drifting off to sleep to the pleasing sounds from the Brit as she attacked the gradients over Shap. It wouldn't have mattered if we had slept through Crewe but one of us shook us all awake to alight there at 05.40. We didn't have too long to wait for a London train as the 74-minute late-running 'Northern Irishman' wasn't far behind and further shuteye was obtained. After commencing my weekend's journey out of Waterloo at 11.30 on the Friday I had accumulated 740 steam miles on thirteen trains – all bar three with required locomotives. Happy days indeed!

The only other occasion I was to travel on the train that year was on Friday 16 September when, having entered Scotland just after 2 a.m. with Brit 70009 *Alfred the Great* on 'The Northern Irishman' and spending a somewhat abortive day searching for steam, Kingmoor's Brit 70005 *John Milton* was turned out. On this occasion I alighted at Carstairs and returned south to Carlisle for a 'guaranteed' Brit worked summer Saturday morning service over Shap. Although having 2 hours to kill at Carlisle, a surfeit of Britannias sheltering from the night under the cavernous roof, blowing off impatiently, helped to pass the time. Present were 70004 *William Shakespeare* and 70018 *Flying Dutchman* waiting for northbound reliefs, 70038 *Robin Hood* on the northbound 'Irishman', whilst my train south, the 23.55 Edinburgh– Birmingham was to be taken forward by 70029 *Shooting Star*. A wonderful scenario if there ever was one, the likes of which will never be witnessed again. Brit 70009 *Alfred the Great* must have been failed at Stranraer, the southbound 'Irishman' being returned into Carlisle at 01.20 by Black 5 45061.

With all enthusiasts mindful that the elimination of steam power throughout Britain was gaining momentum, 1967 was destined to be a very busy year. Personally I was to spend most weekends and over eighty nights away from the home comforts of a warm bed in pursuit of steam! Attention that April was centred in the West Riding with the closure of Leeds Central and the withdrawal of the Bradford portions. On the second Saturday of that month (15th), having spent several unproductive hours at Wakefield, I made my way via Preston (nothing required there either) to Carlisle in the hope, also thwarted, of a new Brit on the Perth train. The foreman that Saturday turned out 70010 *Owen Glendower*, or *Owain Glyndwr* depending upon which side you viewed her, for the 20.32 (which last year's 20.25 had been retimed to) departure which, having achieved 81mph near Wamphray after the station stop at Beattock, breasted the summit in 13 minutes at 55mph. We all alighted at Carstairs that night just making the pub for a few pints of heavy (70s) or light (60s) Scottish beer. To gain entry, the then punitive opening hours dictating a 22.00 closing, required us, because our train was due in at 22.02, to knock on the rear door! After imbibing several pints we returned to Carlisle in the hope of 'something heading south with steam'. This move, however, proved abortive and, although admitting defeat and inevitably ending up on the DL-operated 'Highlander', at least, unlike the previous journey, there was sufficient seating for us. With a mere three catches of steam all day – none of which were required – I could have asked myself was it all worth it? An hour or so after arriving into Euston I was heading north again. I was aboard the Mercian Rail Tour on which I captured haulage with two preserved locomotives: K4 *The Great Marquess* and

Now retimed to depart at 20.32, here are three views of Brit 70022 *Tornado* at Carlisle on Friday 28 April 1967. In the first, no doubt in animated conversation about the catches they had had that day, are two of my lifelong friends, Graham 'Jock' Aitken and Richard 'Joe' Jolliffe – the latter appearing off his own itinerary that day.

In a typically neglected external condition *Tornado*, bereft of nameplates but adorned with a makeshift smokebox number plate, was dispatched to the breaker's yard at the end of that year.

Never judge a book by its cover! *Tornado* was to disrespect the Scottish Region's 75mph speed limit on several occasions that evening.

The logs.

	28/4/61 70022 (2c 2v /)			29/4/67 70012/3c iv /	
Carlisle.	0 00			0 00	
Kingmoor	3 52	52		4 09	45½
Rockcliff	5 51	64		6 35	59
Floriston	7 32	75½/74/73		8 35	61/68
G.J.	9 35	72		10 58	62 / 59
Quintinshill	10 44	74/72		12 30	59½ /70½ msgs 17 03
K'patrick	13 09	73/71		18 04	49
Kirtlebridge	16 09	77½/21		23 26	61/63½/57
Ecclefechan	18 41	77/74		26 50	61/44
Castlemilk R.	20 38	72		29 44 sig.n	61/47
Lockerbie	23 57			39 17	
Nethercleugh	4 01	65		4 12	58½
Dinwoodie	6 35	73		7 24	52½
Wamphray	8 46	76½/82		10 06	64
Murthat	10 37	74		12 20	60
Beattock	13 47			15 57	
MP 41	2 50	38		2 50	40
42	4 20	40		4 15	49½
43	5 49	40		5 36	44½
44	7 20	39½		6 57	46 ... 45
Greskine	09 17	40		8 47	
MP 46	10 17	41½		9 59	42
47	11 42	38½		11 28	38
48	13 18	36		13 07	35
Beattock S	16 09	37		15 24	41/46
Elvanfoot	19 12 pass	65/19		18 16 pass	64/16
Crawford	23 53	70½		29 20	34
Abington	26 37	63/68		26 40	55/49/57
Lamington	31 10	75/73		32 09	69/55½
Symington	33 54	70½/69		35 45	58½
Thankerton	35 23	72½		37 17	71
Leggatfoot	36 43	69		38 49	62/67½
Carstairs	41 30			43 03	

The 20.32 Carlisle–Perth had become, after the ScR authorities had withdrawn all of their home fleet earlier that month, the only regular timetabled passenger train booked for steam haulage within Scotland. Here, on Friday 26 May 1967, Skefko roller bearing equipped Black 5 44674, deputising for a failed Brit, awaits departure time at Carlisle. This Kingmoor-allocated locomotive failed to survive the massacre upon the shed's closure seven months later.

A3 *Flying Scotsman*. So the answer would have been yes, of course. That frenetic period, in the mid 1960s, of chasing the steam locomotive throughout Britain can never be replicated and, although at the time I did question my sanity, I'm glad to have accomplished as much travelling as my stamina permitted. For the football followers amongst the readers, Scotland had beaten England 3-2 in the European Championship qualifying round at Wembley that Saturday.

Aware that it was the final Friday of Scottish steam, a pre-planned trip with lifelong friend Graham (Jock) to the disappointingly few remaining steam-hauled Glasgow suburban trains on Friday 28 April (fully detailed in the following chapter) resulted in the pair of us cutting our losses and heading south to Carlisle for the 20.32 departure. Kingmoor turned out 70022 *Tornado* that night and, being a Friday, the load was increased, with an empty sleeping car, to four! The best run yet was, however, obtained with a maximum of 81mph approaching Ecclefechan, 82mph just after Wamphray, breasting the summit at 37mph before achieving 71mph at Thankerton: 73½ miles of sheer delight, seriously exceeding the 75mph Scottish Region imposed maximum for steam! Having alighted at Carstairs for a few bevvies (indeed the co-operative landlord at The Carstairs Junction Hotel had stated that if advised by phone that we were coming he would line up a considerable number of pints in readiness for our arrival!), we headed south to Leeds to catch the final steam departure out of the Central: 44846 on the 03.32 departure for Halifax. By the early afternoon, having exhausted the NER for required catches, what did we do? Why, return to Carlisle (encompassing a 2½-hour DMU ride over the Long Drag) for the 20.32 Perth departure, of course! Retimed to start (because of engineering work) at 21.10, Brit 70012 *John of Gaunt* was provided for the Saturday train but, in comparison to the previous day's exploits, it was a disappointment, with a maximum of a mere 78mph near Symington. On this occasion, because of the revised timings, we couldn't partake of liquid refreshment at Carstairs – just making (on paper) a cross platform minus 2-minute connection, thus enabling us, upon arrival into London, to then enjoy a further 216 steam miles travelling out of Waterloo on the 09.33 excursion train to Bournemouth with the now preserved *Clan Line*.

Three weeks later, with The Tremeloes' 'Silence is Golden' beginning its three-week stint at the top spot, Saturday 20 May found me on the K1-powered Three Dales Rail Tour. Alighting at Darlington, I made my way via Newcastle to Carlisle for 70023 *Venus*'s turn on the train noting, when passing Beattock, that the banking duties were now provided by English Electric Type 1s (Class 20) – Black 5MT 45319 of Motherwell and Standard tank 80086 of Polmadie in open store there. It was to be expected, Scotland's steam fleet having been massacred only weeks earlier. Travel on this train through the diesel desert Scotland had become now seemed all the more adventurous – or should that read precarious! This train was now unique in being the only regular timetabled all-year passenger train booked for steam haulage within Scotland. How much longer would it continue to be steam operated? Aware of a 1X89 Parspec departure south from Carlisle later that night, we alighted at Carstairs, returning there as quickly as possible. Having seen Brit 70016 *Ariel* hook up to the front of the train for some reason, not entered into my tattered notebook, we were unable to board – locked doors, alert party organiser, police presence, who knows? Serves them right (my notebook did say): a 55-minute delay was incurred due to water ingress in the steam pipe! Returning south on the ever-reliable 'Northern Irishman' and, having noted a Brush Type 4 on the 09.33 Waterloo excursion to Bournemouth, I unexpectedly, from my parents' point of view, returned home that weekend far earlier than usual.

On 25 May that year Celtic became the first British team to reach a European Cup Final and also to win it, beating Inter Milan 2-1 in Portugal. Politically the outspoken Tory MP Enoch Powell had described Britain as 'the sick man of Europe' – an attack on the sitting Labour government. It was to be a further eleven months before his controversial Rivers of Blood speech was made at Birmingham protesting against the 1968 Race Relation Act. At the end of that May was a Scottish Fair weekend. This led to a plethora of extras and, with ownership of the appropriate LMR STN on Friday the 26th, we were able to cross the border on three occasions behind steam within 17 hours: at 03.30, 18.00 and 20.40. The last crossing of the day was of course aboard the 20.32 Carlisle–Perth train with Skefko bearing equipped Black 5MT 44674 standing in at short notice for a Brit failure. On this occasion, after having utilised the 30-minute pathing stop at Carstairs to quaff a few pints, we then returned to the train and continued to Coatbridge where, appetites whetted, the late-night chippy was once again visited during the 43 minutes available prior to the arrival of the southbound 'Highlander'. Oh how we lived back then!

The following day, having caught Brit 70038 *Robin Hood* on one of the extras into Glasgow Central at 19.06, we headed to Lanark, the intention being to intercept the Carlisle–Perth train at Carstairs. With the railway between Lanark and Carstairs having closed the previous year I, at the time, made no notes as to how we completed the journey. When Jock proofread this book, he recalled that we had two taxis take us between the two stations. Two, I queried? Yes – there were seven of us! What ends would we go to back then – all for a measly 21¼ miles of Brit 10 haulage to Coatbridge!

Finally heading south once again on the crowded 'Highlander', we changed on to 'The Northern Irishman' at Carlisle in the hope, subsequently justified, of a bed for the night on an emptier train. For the football followers amongst the readers, league leaders Celtic had beaten Aberdeen 2-0 in the Scottish FA Cup Final that weekend.

Not satisfied with the substantial steam mileage of 758 already accumulated that weekend, on bank holiday Monday 29 May (the first spring bank holiday replacing, in England and Wales, the former Whitsun) I ventured north once more and caught the 20.32 to Carlisle for, retrospectively, my last occasion. Brit 70038 *Robin Hood* again powered the train. Presumably, as it was the end of the Glasgow Fair weekend, the amount of passengers joining at Lockerbie completely overwhelmed the two-coach train and all corridors were fully occupied! I had already booked the Tuesday off and, having returned to Carlisle during the early hours of that morning, I boarded the 05.32 Barrow departure for an 86-mile 3-hour bone-shaking DMU journey via the scenic Cumberland coast. This was to connect into the 08.35 London departure which on that day, rather than attach at Lancaster to a Carlisle–Euston train, ran in its own right as a separate train. 70027 *Rising Star* provided a further 106¾ steam miles to Crewe.

Moving on to July and, with The Beatles' 'All You Need Is Love' holding sway at the top of the charts, the first colour transmission on television, coverage of the Wimbledon men's final, was broadcast on Saturday the 1st. On that day, to avoid full-on depression in connection with the impending demise of steam on my home patch (SR), I travelled to Carlisle on the 13.20 Euston–Glasgow Central. It was the first running of that service that summer and unsure what was going to be steam or diesel was much relieved upon seeing Brit 70025 *Western Star* reversing round the corner at Crewe to work the 141 miles over Shap. Upon arriving into Carlisle I was in a position, so to speak, to travel on the 20.32 Perth departure should it have been steam. A Sulzer Type 2 was gurgling away at its head. As confirmed in a LCGB bulletin some time later, booked steam on regular all-year timetabled trains into Scotland had ended, but I will be forever indebted to having participated in travelling aboard, on nine separate occasions, that Perth service.

15

THE FINAL WEEKEND

HAVING DETAILED THE unique Britannia-worked Perth starter out of Carlisle until its dieselisation in June 1967, perhaps now is the time to document what else had happened during those first six months elsewhere in Scotland. The first shed to close to steam, in the February, was St Margarets, with Ferryhill following suit the next month. The final V2, 60836, lived on having been moved from Dundee to Craigentinny Carriage Sidings, Edinburgh – the mundane task of steam heating coaches not necessarily befitting its once majestic status. A grand Easter rail tour was run, formed of a substantial eighteen vehicles, using Perth's final solitary locomotive, Black 5MT 44997 and the now preserved A4 60009 *Union of South Africa*, both of which operated the Perth–Aberdeen and Perth–Edinburgh sections of the tour.

Moving on to the scheduled timetabled services, 'The Northern Irishman' was now two Type 2 DLs (Class 25) Stranraer–Carlisle and return. The same pair were booked in and out of Carlisle with a mere 30-minute turnaround – needless to say, a Brit often stood in on the northbound to Ayr due to late running! Both the 09.20 and 19.44 Waverley-routed Carlisle–Edinburgh departures were sporadically reported as being steam worked and Jubilee 45647 *Sturdee* unusually worked from Glasgow to Carlisle on the Good Friday. Also at Easter, Kingmoor's 8F 48602 (vice a Brit) worked a Northwich–Larbert soda ash train into Scotland, all Scottish sheds having sent their own 8Fs over the border in October 1963. Finally the Brit off the 20.32 Carlisle was sent by the Perth foreman to Edinburgh on the 06.47 departure on at least three occasions that April.

S C O T L A N D

NOTE: All steam services in Scotland are expected to finish at the end of this year.

B I S H O P T O N

1822 SX	To Glasgow Central	5MT

C A R L I S L E

2025	To Perth	7MT	12A

G L A S G O W   C E N T R A L

0655 SX	To Hillington	5MT
0719 SX	To Renfrew Wharf	4MTT
0822 SX	To Gourock	4MTT
1557 SX	To Gourock	4MTT
1654 SX	To Gourock	4MTT

G O U R O C K

1703 SX	To Glasgow Central	4MTT
1740 SX	To Glasgow Central	4MTT
1915 SX	To Glasgow Central	4MTT

P A I S L E Y   C A N A L

0755 SX	To Glasgow Central	5MT

P E R T H

1900	To Aberdeen	5MT
2203	To Dundee	5MT

Colleague Roger Price had written to all the regions requesting details of their steam worked passenger trains. Upon appreciating that all profits were to go to the SR Children's Orphanage at Woking they willingly supplied the information. Here is an extract showing the booked steam services in Scotland in early 1967.

Returning to my travels, the dateline being Thursday 27 April 1967, and having been aboard a wonderfully exhilarating 101mph run with Merchant Navy 35003 *Royal Mail* on a Salisbury–Waterloo train earlier that evening, Jock and I made our way over to Euston for the 21.25 departure for Scotland. It was the final weekend of Scottish-allocated steam and we were making one last attempt to catch some steam runs on the Glasgow Central's suburban services. Having arrived into Glasgow Central at 06.15 on the Friday morning, we didn't have long to wait with Corkerhill's Black 5 44699 working that day's 06.55 departure for Hillington West – a station just 5 miles along the Gourock line. The most recent documentation in our possession in regard to steam passenger services north of the border indicated both this and the following 07.19 Glasgow Central to Renfrew Wharf as being steam operated and, sure enough, after a mere 24-minute wait a very clean 67A-allocated Standard tank, 80004, arrived with the 07.19 ex Glasgow.

This branch, originally opened in 1837 and built to the Scotch gauge of 4ft 6in, was constructed to compete with the transportation of passengers and goods on the nearby River Cart between Paisley and the River Clyde – Glasgow-bound passengers completing their journeys by riverboat. In 1842, to save money, it switched to horse haulage – the nearby recently opened Paisley Gilmour Street railway having siphoned off much of its passenger traffic. In January 1866 passenger services were suspended, the line doubled, regauged to standard and, after a connecting spur to the main line at Paisley was inaugurated, reopened four months later. The closure of Clyde shipyards during the early 1960s led to a fall in traffic and the branch was subsequently listed in the Beeching proposals for closure. Reference to the timetable showed the train we were on that morning was the only one serving Renfrew Wharf itself each SX day. The sole returning branch train, the 16.41, started back from Renfrew Fulbar Street, which was ½ mile distant! With this not exactly customer-friendly service on offer, the inevitable closure came that June. With the stock presumably being stabled in this weed-infested site (allegedly Renfrew Wharf station) for the day, we somehow (bus or taxi?) got to Paisley Gilmour Street in time for the 08.22 Glasgow–Gourock service (expected to be steam but wasn't) before making our way back to Glasgow Central to sample the delights of a Travellers Fare (station buffet) breakfast.

The next allegedly booked steam departure was the 15.57 for Gourock and, although by genre we were categorised as 'haulage chasers', to fill the day we made an unfamiliar decision to go shed bashing. After catching the 10.13 DMU to Corkerhill, 'Turn left outside the station along Corkerhill Place. About 200 yards further on a cinder path leads from the left-hand side of the road (by the Railway Mission Building) to the shed. Walking time 5 minutes.' We first visited 67A where, excluding withdrawn Standard tank 80128, the only locomotive in steam was one of the two that had given us a ride earlier that day – Black 5 44699. I didn't document how we reached our next shed, 66A Polmadie, but no doubt my good friend's knowledge of his own country's transport system,

This, together with the following four photographs, was taken on the final Friday of Scottish steam – 28 April 1967. Somewhere here, amongst the overgrown vegetation, was Renfrew Wharf station. The 07.19 from Glasgow Central was powered on this, its last steam-worked day, by Corkerhill's Standard 4MT 80004. The train itself went DMU from the following Monday, until the line's closure five weeks later.

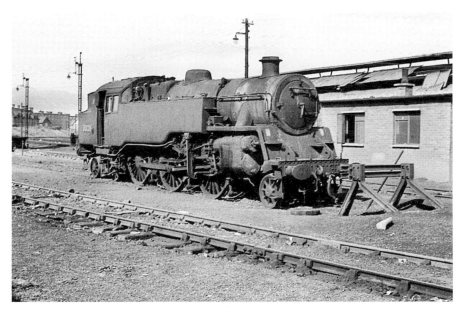

Already withdrawn Standard 4MT 80128 awaits her fate at Corkerhill shed – her home for eleven of her eleven and a half years of existence.

Motherwell allocated but seen here at Polmadie was Scotland's sole surviving LMS tank: Derby-built 20-year-old 42274. She was specially diagrammed to work an 'end of steam' 17.03 Gourock–Glasgow Central that evening, but not being aware of it and also frustrated by the lack of steam earlier that rush hour we were en route south by then!

One of the by then six remaining Standard 4MTs (in Scotland), 11-year-old Brighton-built 80116, is in light steam at Polmadie (66A) shed. Once the home of Stanier's Pacifics for the WCML services out of Glasgow Central, the deserted and neglected scenario associated with steam sheds in their dying days is portrayed to great effect here.

A representative of a class of locomotive never allocated in Scotland is BR 9F 2-10-0 92051 of Kingmoor. Seen visiting Motherwell shed (66B), she was withdrawn that November, aged just 12 years old.

several buses and a lot of shoe leather were involved. Here eleven locomotives were 'copped' as follows: in steam: 42274, 44796, 70012 *John of Gaunt* (12A), 73059, 73060, 80116 and 80120; dead: 45124, 73064, 73079 and 80045.

Having somehow returned to Glasgow Central, we boarded the 13.53 EMU for Motherwell ('Turn left outside the station along Muir Street (main road). Turn right after crossing the railway bridge. This is a rough cul-de-sac and the shed entrance is at the end. Walking time: 10 minutes') and 66B was arrived at. A grand total of four locomotives awaited our attention; in steam: 44991 and 92051 (12A); dead: 45167 and 73146.

Returning once more into Glasgow, our expectations of the evening's steam-worked services soon evaporated, catching 'Chopper' D8124 on the 15.57 Gourock* service the 12 miles out to Bishopton and returning on the 16.22 starting service with Sulzer Type 2 D5363. Both trains were supposedly rostered for steam! That's it – totally disillusioned we'd had enough of waiting around and departed for the fifth and final time that day out of Glasgow Central – this time with D1853 on the 17.25 for Carlisle. We passed Carstairs (66E) en route

---

* Had we stayed on this train, due in Gourock at 16.54, we would have seen it form the 17.03 return service which was worked by Scotland's last remaining Fairburn, 42274, seen at Polmadie that morning.

noting a solitary 70010 *Owen Glendower* (12A) in situ. Unaware, at the time, of the paucity of steam available in Scotland, we had actually 'copped' 50 per cent of Scotland's final allocation! Nancy and Frank Sinatra's 'Somethin' Stupid' was topping the charts that week; having spent an abortive day chasing non-existent steam trains, the comparison was unintentionally appropriate.

Listed below are the thirty remaining Scottish steam-allocated locomotives as on Monday 1 May 1967. All except 65288 (62C) and 65345 (62A) were condemned that day and although the two J36s were not (officially?) withdrawn until 5 June the two sheds at which they were allocated are documented as having closed to steam on 1 May.

Shed	Locomotives
62A Thornton Junction	65345
62B Dundee (Tay Bridge)	61072, 61180
62C Dunfermline	65288
63A Perth	44997
66A Polmadie (Glasgow)	44796, 45124, 73059, 73060, 73064. 73079, 76104, 80045, 80086, 80116, 80120
66B Motherwell	42274, 44991, 45167, 45319, 45359, 45423, 73146, 76000
66F Beattock	76094, 76098
67A Corkerhill (Glasgow)	44699, 76046, 80004, 80046

For the football aficionados amongst the readers, Celtic and Rangers topped Division One that year with Morton and Raith Rovers heading up Division Two.

27th April 1967

via 8MY/VA			1¾
0816	Clapham Junction	✓ 82019	3½
0824	Kensington (Olympia)	✓ —	-
0833	Kensington (Olympia)	4E 82019	3½
0841	Clapham Junction	SE —	-
via WM./WORK			3
1653	Wimbledon	1L NR	17
1721	Woking	5L —	-
1734	Woking	1E D867*	42
1833	Andover	2L —	-
1906	Andover	1E 35003	44½
2036	Waterloo	2L —	-
2125	Euston	✓ E3102	150½

28th April 1967

↓	Crewe	D1844*	141
0319	Carlisle	1AE —	
0344	Carlisle	5L D1843 *	
0610	Glasgow Central	6L —	102½
0655	Glasgow Central	✓ 44699*	5
0710	Hillington West	2E —	
0734	Hillington West	✓ 80004*	5
0756	Renfrew Wharf	4E —	
0839	Paisley Gilmour St.	✓ NR	7½
0852	Glasgow Central	✓ —	-
1003	Glasgow Central	✓ NR	7½
1013	Corkerhill	✓ —	-
1353	Glasgow Central	✓ NR	14½

Cert
ST 2 8 / 5 8 / 3 9 / 4 1 / 1 3 / 3 6
42274 ECS / 80116 ECS / D8124 ~ 1823
NR 17
had shown to Renfrew Wharf

1429	Motherwell	04E —	-
1504	Motherwell	✓ NR	14½
1538	Glasgow Central	✓ —	-
1557	Glasgow Buchanan St	1E D8124*	12¾
1617	Bishopton	1L —	-
1622	Bishopton	✓ D5363*	12¾
1647	Glasgow Central	2L —	-
1725	Glasgow Central	7L D1853	102½
1925	Carlisle	3L —	-
2038	Carlisle	8L 70022	73½
2202	Carstairs	✓ —	-
2240	Carstairs	✓ D1841*	73½

29th April 1967

0004	Carlisle	5L —	-
0046	Carlisle	✓ D11 *	113
0300	Leeds City	3L —	-
0332	Leeds Central	✓ 44846*	16½
0402	Halifax	✓ —	-
0438	Halifax	✓ 44846	8¾
0505	Hebden Bridge	2E —	
0528	Hebden Bridge	✓ 45219*	27½
0650	Normanton	✓ —	
0712	Normanton	✓ D83*	10
0731	Cudworth	✓ —	
0758	Cudworth	2L 45075	21
0851	Leeds City	1L —	
0917	Leeds City	6L D7570*	13½
0943	Bradford Forster Sq.	3L —	-

Notebook extract of that Friday visit.

An extract from the August 1967 issue of the LCGB bulletin. (With thanks to the LCGB organisation)

SCOTTISH REGION

The use of steam on passenger trains in Scotland came to an abrupt halt as from 5th June. This has been achieved by a change in the region's provision of power for trains running north to Carlisle. Previously, power for most relief and seasonal trains running north of Carlisle would be provided by Kingmoor in the form of Class 5's and Britannias (see page 143, July Bulletin for an example). As from 5th June the Scottish Region took over this responsibility, hence power now varies from BR/Sulzer Type 2's to LMR Type 4's on fill-in turns.

One regular train was affected by the change, the 20.32 Carlisle to Perth, now a Type 2 working.

Steam is still used on seasonal and relief trains south of Carlisle, but the only way to continue north is when a diesel fails or one is not available. Such trains are now few, due to steam heating not being required (the usual cause of diesel failures), whilst an increasing number of diesel locos are available as standbys. Failures which steam replaced recently included:

26th June: 21.25 Euston - Perth, D1850 failed at Carlisle, 70031 working forward.

22nd June: 19.44 Carlisle - Edinburgh was worked by 70045.
20.32 Carlisle - Perth has been steam hauled on several occasions since 5th June.

✗ SCOTTISH REGION (4 Weeks Ended 27/5/67)

WITHDRAWN: (1/5/67) 42274 66B, 44699 67A, 44796 66A, 44991 66B, 44997 63A, 45124 66A, 45167/319/59/423 66B, 61072/180 62B, 73059/60/4/79/146 66A, 76000 66B, 76046 67A, 76094/8 66F, 76104 66A, 80004 67A, 80045 66A, 80046 67A, 80086/116/20 66A.

TRANSFERS: D2415 - 9 64H, D2587 61A, D2589/90 64H, D2593 62C, D2595/6 64H, D2597 61A, D2608/17 62C, D2618 64H.

INTER-REGIONAL TRANSFERS: From ER 12107 (7/5) 64B then 62A, D1994 (7/5) 66A (OL).

Note: The above withdrawals end the steam allocations of the Motive Power Depots at Dundee (Tay Bridge) (62B), Perth (63A), Polmadie (66A), Motherwell (66B), Beattock (66F) and Corkerhill (67A).

16

AND STILL THEY COME

SO WAS THAT IT? I am certain the Scottish Region authorities could never have foreseen the foreman's predilection at the one-time Scottish shed of Carlisle Kingmoor for dispatching wave after wave of steam penetrations over the border after the home fleet was withdrawn that May. Unwanted and unwelcome, they were usually dispatched light engine back over the border post-haste. The final booked all-year steam penetration, that of the Carlisle–Perth, was diagrammed for DL haulage just weeks later.

The January 1967 steam allocation at 12A was still a creditable 114 – the dominant classes being Black 5s (forty-seven), Brits (thirty-four) and 9Fs (twenty-four). The Brit allocation, the previous month, had been bolstered with Upperby dispatching all their mechanically fit examples upon its closure – indeed only five (70000, 26, 30, 43 and 4) were never allocated at Kingmoor. Whilst representatives of other steam classes were still alive elsewhere, 12A became the Britannia's graveyard. They had all migrated from various locations throughout Britain to the LMR; the only escapee of the December 1967 massacre was the subsequently preserved *Oliver Cromwell*.

As briefly touched upon earlier, the last weekend of May 1967 was a public holiday in Scotland and produced a welter of specials from London and Birmingham. Suitably equipped with the necessary LMR STNs, we – Jock and I – homed in on them, accumulating over 1,000 steam miles within four days, of which 775 were behind Brits. Unsure which of them would be steam, we positioned ourselves at Crewe in the early hours of Friday 26th. We didn't have to wait long: the 35-minute late-running 22.07 (relief) Euston–Glasgow was departing at 01.05 with Brit 70022 *Tornado*. At Carlisle, however, when

Some of the tickets used during my adventures.

70025 *Western Star* replaced her after a seemingly lengthy time she was declared a failure (brakes) and, together with several vehicles, was detached and sent away. She was replaced by sister 70016 *Ariel*. This was the first of nine occasions that weekend that I was either to pass through or stop off at Carlisle. Arriving into Glasgow 80 minutes late, at 07.22, we nonchalantly strolled round to board the 07.35 Euston departure that returned us to Crewe to await the next batch of Scotland–bound specials.

With less than half an hour's wait there, we took 44802 on the 12.30 (relief) Crewe–Glasgow as far as Preston, where the opportunity to consume food and

SCOTTISH REGION

The Scottish Region became the third region on British Rail to eliminate steam power as from 1st May, 1967. Depots which used steam prior to this date have stored their allocation, usually outside the shed.

The loco hauled Gourock trains have been taken over by type 1 and 2 diesels until the electric services start on 5th June.

Banking duties at Beattock are covered by English Electric type 1s.

Kingmoor's steam locos continue to work north of the border. The 20.32 Carlisle - Perth continues a Britannia working, but servicing facilities are due to be withdrawn from Perth as from 5th June, so its future as a steam train seems doubtful.

The loco arriving at Perth off the 20.32 ex Carlisle continued to find itself on the 06.43 Perth - Edinburgh the next day. 70013 for instance was used on 27th April.

The 12.10 T.Th.O Corkickle - Coatbridge iron ore train is diagrammed for a class 9F 2-10-0+Class 5 4-6-0 north of Carlisle.

Preserved A.4 "Sir Nigel Gresley" returned to Scotland to work a rail tour on 20th May, from Glasgow Central to Aberdeen. The outward route was via Stirling and Forfar, returning via Dundee, Dunfermline and the Forth Bridge. The Pacific worked north on the 13.28 Crewe - Carlisle parcels on 16th May, continuing the next day on the 18.10 Carlisle - Glasgow Parcels Station.

On the last day of steam at Dundee, 28th April, only nine locos were on shed including 60532. The only locos seen in steam were 61102 and 61072 which were shunting in the goods yard.

Steam heating duties at Edinburgh up to the end of May at least, were covered by 61180. 60836 and 45483 which were used previously, are now stored at Thornton Jc.

Relief trains to Scotland via the West Coast were almost monopolized by steam power during the few days before the Spring Bank Holiday. Workings at Carlisle were as follows:

			CARLISLE arr.	dep.
25th May				
1X07	12.30	Crewe - Glasgow	70010	70046
26th May				
1X07	22.05	(25th) Euston - Glasgow	70022	70016
1X04	12.30	Crewe - Glasgow	44802	700XX
1X09	12.10	Euston - Perth	44832	44795
1X05	13.40	Euston - Glasgow	70028	70038
1X06	15.42	Euston - Glasgow	44669	45212
27th May				
1X28	22.05	(26th) Euston - Glasgow	70027	70028
1X30	23.05	(26th) Euston - Glasgow	700XX	70039
1X29	23.30	(26th) Birmingham - Edinburgh	Brush Type 4	
1S46	09.00	Liverpool - Glasgow	Brush Type 4	
1S52	06.40	Birmingham - Glasgow	44675	D1874
1S62	11.35	Birmingham - Edinburgh	70045	D1974
1S37	09.20	St. Pancras - Glasgow	D78	70038

1X09 on 26th did not change locos at Motherwell, the usual practice for this train, but was worked through to Perth by 44795. The very next train to reach Perth behind the relief was a northbound freight, also hauled by a class 5, No. 45437 !

An extract from the July 1967 LCGB bulletin. (With thanks to the LCGB organisation)

No health and safety restrictions back then! I had alighted from the 12.10 (relief) Euston–Perth here at Lockerbie on Friday 26 May 1967 and raced along the embankment to obtain these shots of lifelong Kingmoor resident Stanier 4-6-0 44795's departure. Every penetration into the diesel desert of Scotland had become worthy of recording.

drink was taken advantage of, before the 12.10 (relief) Euston–Perth with 44832 (5B) took us over Shap to Carlisle. With sister 44795 taking over, we reboarded the train to its first calling point of Lockerbie – a town where in 1988 a Pam Am flight crashed following a terrorist bomb killing 270. We didn't have too long to wait for a southbound service returning us to Carlisle, conveniently connecting us into the old favourite 20.32 Perth departure.

Returning south on 'The Royal Highlander' and with time to kill before Saturday's lunchtime batch of reliefs out of Crewe, Caprotti Standard 5MT 73132 (9H) was taken into Manchester on the 05.45 Wigan detachment of sleepers before returning to the WCML for a Barrow–Euston extra, 70005 *John Milton* taking us south to Crewe. It took a great deal of planning to encompass as many of the extras as possible but it came naturally to us as both our careers had morphed from telephone call centre operatives into the BR planning departments. The only aspect we couldn't control was whether the intended trains were steam or diesel. Fortune was on our side, however, when, after about an hour's wait, Brit 70045 *Lord Rowallan* was turned out for a Birmingham–Edinburgh relief train. Taken over at Carlisle by a diesel, salvation came when a 09.20 (relief) St Pancras–Glasgow, having come over the Midland route from Leeds, was worked forward via the G&SWR with 70038 *Robin Hood*. After making our way over to Carstairs for the 20.32 former Carlisle, we finally headed home to London on the ever-reliable 'Highlander'.

The reader might, at this point, question the author's sanity in travelling so extensively in such a short space of time. In my defence there were still five more Brits that I had yet to have a run with: 70014, 5, 21, 35 and 9. The first three had been allocated at Stockport and were reportedly, according to fellow gricers, stored at the closed Upperby shed, but with the ever-changing steam scene you never knew whether it was still the case. The reality was that *Iron Duke* and *Morning Star* were indeed returned to service and by the penultimate Saturday of the summer service I caught a run behind both; *Apollo* was missed, having been condemned upon arrival at Kingmoor.

One of the most pleasurable occurrences while chasing steam in those halcyon days during those final years were the unexpected turn ups which resulted in the complete revision of any plans already made. It was the third weekend of July 1967 and, having spent the day on WCML services in the Preston area, I was at Wigan North Western station at just gone midnight looking forward, albeit after a near 3-hour fester there, to putting my head down on the southbound 'Highlander' en route home. I didn't possess a copy of the LMR STN that weekend and was therefore completely unaware that a Paignton–Glasgow relief was booked to call there; upon feasting my eyes on the motive power,

Waiting for a Scotland-bound train at Crewe, some of my travelling mates from those wonderful far off days: (l–r) Barry Reed, myself (Wild Bill), Les 'Lurch' Kent, Roger Price (author of typewritten issues), Pete Bowyer and Graham 'Jock' Aitken. (Alan Nobby Hayes)

Notebook extract detailing just another weekend jaunt; 1,021¼ of the 3,073¾ miles were steam hauled.

I dashed hell for leather along the platform, under the subway, just making the train before its departure north. Why the rush? I just couldn't refuse a train double header with a pair of Stanier's finest: 44758 (10A) and 44878 (12A).

This was a true act of a haulage basher. Once aboard, only then did I look into the consequences of my action. Although the train briefly stopped at Preston, I reasoned that, as the southbound 'Highlander' was not calling there, I would have been stranded for a great many hours, and the lure of a warm comfortable compartment was preferable to the hard benches of a waiting room. I had been on the go since leaving work on the Friday afternoon and the sleep deprivation took effect almost immediately upon departing Preston; it was only the DL coupling on to the front at Carlisle upon arrival there some 2½ hours later that disturbed me enough to alight.

What now? The next train south was the 09.55 departure. Some time later Brit 70024 *Vulcan* came up LE from Kingmoor and sat tantalisingly in the middle road – for what? As already stated, I wasn't privy to any special notices that particular weekend so when a 21.20 (relief) St Pancras–Glasgow came in with a Peak DL only to be uncoupled for *Vulcan* to take forward, I thought 'why not?' – steam into Glasgow was becoming pretty rare. I was now fully awake and ready to enjoy yet another dawn entry into Scotland and, unsure of its routing, realised at Gretna that it was taking the G&SWR route via Dumfries. With an added attraction of travelling via Dalry and Paisley (engineering work diversion?), an arrival time of 08.08 at Glasgow Central was achieved.

Reference to the timetable showed the quickest way home was on the 10.00 Edinburgh Waverley–King's Cross and so, having walked the walk to Glasgow's only other remaining railway terminus – Queen Street – a Sunday morning DMU across to Edinburgh was undertaken. Having secured a seat aboard the King's Cross train just prior to departure, an announcement over the PA system was made to the effect that due to a derailment at Acklington (Northumberland) the train was to be diverted. Oh well, I thought, at least I wouldn't suffer a bus journey en route and, with a right time departure, Deltic D9017 *The Durham Light Infant* headed eastwards before unexpectedly, to me, veering right off the ECML at Portobello Junction to head south over the Waverley route – a line over which I had yet to travel. The North British Railway drew inspiration from Melrose resident Sir Walter Scott's novels, thus conferring to the route the appellation of the Waverley Line.

Most Class 1 expresses and fast freights over this route were once monopolised by Gresley's A3s, with B1s, D49s and V2s playing their part on the semis. The long-distance freight services were usually V2s – the stopping passenger trains utilising J39 0-6-0 and BR Standard 4MT 2-6-0s. After Canal shed's clo-cure in 1963, all passenger services over this route were booked for DL power; I was never present when a failure caused a replacement steam alternative to be dispatched by either the St Margarets or Kingmoor foreman.

Constructed by the North British Railway, the 53-mile section of the line north of Hawick was opened in 1849; the remaining 45 miles south over the Scottish lowlands was not completed until thirteen years later. The route was famous for its significant gradients and bleak moorland terrain which proved taxing for both the steam locomotives and their crews to master. The climb started immediately at Portobello Junction and steepened after Eskbank, 8 miles into the journey, to nearly 10 miles of 1 in 70. Having surmounted the summit at Falahill (878ft), it then descended at a kinder 1 in 150 through Galashiels and Melrose. It is here, between those two stations, that, on 6 September 2015, train services have returned to the line from Edinburgh, terminating at the newly constructed station of Tweedbank.

The majority of services over the line in the 1960s were stopping services and the novelty factor of a timetabled train running non-stop over the double-tracked route that morning was not wasted on me. The Waverley route had an overall speed limit of 70mph, although there were a great many restrictions over tight curves. The scenery, so far, had been awesome – but the best was yet to come. The next 15 miles to Hawick* was almost level before the 11-mile climb, some of which was at 1 in 75, to the highest point, at 1,006ft above sea level, of the line at Whitrope summit. After passing through the 1,206-yard Whitrope Tunnel, the line then descended for 8 miles at an unbroken 1 in 75 through the isolated Riccarton Junction, Steele Road and Newcastleton stations, after which an easier ride into Carlisle completed the 98-mile journey.

During the mania years the line spawned myriad connectional branch lines – perhaps just one of the junction stations deserving a special mention. Riccarton Junction, constructed in the heart of the Lees Bog, was in the middle of nowhere. Prior to the railways coming, apart from a remote shepherd's bothy, there were no buildings or inhabitants in the area. The railway bought its own community in the form of Riccarton railway village, comprising terraced housing, a shop on the station platform and a school. The new community (which peaked at 180), 1½ miles from the nearest road, had no doctor so a locomotive was kept permanently in steam at Hawick to convey emergency services to the village when required. Initially Sunday worshippers used the

---

*   The withdrawal of train services from Hawick in 1969 gave the town the unenviable accolade of being the largest town in the UK (2011 census = 14,294) furthest from a railway station. The opening of Tweedbank, however, has remedied that situation, being a mere 17 miles distant.

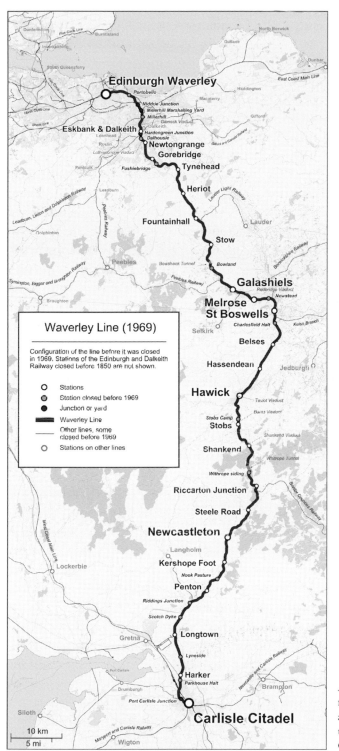

A 1969 Waverley route map. (© Penchristener and licensed for reuse under the Creative Commons Licence)

engine shed, then the waiting room, a minister walking from Saughtree on the adjoining Border counties line to officiate the services. Eventually church trains were provided to take worshippers to Newcastleton and Hawick on Sundays.

I was famished, after all I should have been home by now, and so counting up all my pennies I found I had enough to afford lunch aboard the 8-hour journey, espying while tucking into my roast beef, at Durran Hill, 60019 *Bittern* on an A4 tour from Leeds to Glasgow. I eventually arrived home some 12 hours later than planned.

A mere six days later, and having exhausted any possibility of new haulages within the NER, I travelled to Carlisle over Ais Gill with Holbeck's Jubilee 45593 *Kolhapur* – the intention being to then head south over Shap to the steam-infested Preston area.The train concerned was the 06.40 Birmingham–Glasgow and, having suffered over an hour's delay en route at Wath North (DL failure), it was actually just gone 2 p.m. upon arriving into Carlisle. Although I believed at the time that the train was booked for DL haulage forward, over the years I have seen several prints in the railway press showing various Kingmoor Black 5s working it in Scotland.That aside, after a lengthy period a chime whistle announced the recently transferred in, from Stockport, Brit 70021 *Morning Star* reversing slowly on to the train. For some reason (family commitment perhaps?) I wasn't planning to stay out a second night that week-end and, confronted with my penultimate requirement of a much-wanted Brit, frantic page turning of timetables resulted in me reboarding the train to its first stop at Dumfries, a 12-minute connection returning me home just after midnight.

A further six days later, on Friday 28 July, I booked a day's annual leave specifically to travel on the, hopefully still steam-operated, 13.27 FSO Manchester–Glasgow service. Although the train was Brit hauled south of Carlisle, 70032 *Tennyson* having replaced failed sister 70010 at Carnforth, the train was disappointingly DL hauled over the border. So I abandoned the train and, with the next known steam-hauled departure being the 02.22 for Crewe, I was about to return south when Black 5 44964 arrived in with a Euston–Perth relief train. It was one of those right time, right place scenarios when no sooner than 44964 came off the train Kingmoor's 45455 backed on. As she was a required locomotive I was aboard before you could say 'Bob's your uncle' – irrespective of where the first call was going to be.The ScR authorities must have been fed up to the back teeth with Kingmoor continuously forwarding steam over the border into their diesel desert and had decreed, by that date, that no steam was to continue north of Glasgow. This edict meant Black 5 45455 was replaced at Motherwell by a Brush Type 4, which caused me to alight and return to England via Glasgow.

After a lengthy delay at Carlisle Brit 70021 *Morning Star* was requisitioned to work the 06.40 Birmingham New Street–Glasgow Central forward on Saturday 22 July 1967. Seen here departing from Dumfries, she had, by that date, became one of my few required Brits – being a former Stockport transferee.

The Scottish Region authorities were progressively clamping down of steam incursions being sent out by the Kingmoor foreman and by this date, Friday 28 July 1967, had made Motherwell the most northerly point on the WCML they were allowed to go. Here long-term 12A resident 29-year-old Stanier workhorse 45455 is seen being detached from the 12.10 (relief) Euston–Perth at Motherwell, no doubt, as usual, returning LE home.

Steam into Scotland, although not uncommon, was not to be sniffed at and, having spotted in the LMR STN notices a 13.52 Euston–Glasgow relief running on Friday 11 August, considered it a fair enough bet to take a half-day's leave for. After surmounting (unassisted) Shap with Kingmoor's 44899, this eight-vehicle train was relinquished to Brit 70032 *Tennyson* at Carlisle for the 116½-mile journey over former G&SWR metals, arriving a mere 17 minutes late into Glasgow at 22.10. This was to become my last steam into Glasgow and, having returned south to Carlisle for the following morning's 02.22 Brit-worked departure for Crewe, I spent the remainder of that weekend, as all others after that date, on WCML services south of Lancaster.

The final public timetabled passenger service booked for steam out of Carlisle and over Shap, on 16 September 1967, was the 02.22 Birmingham departure, worked that morning by Brit 70032 *Tennyson*. I was on the train a week earlier with sister *Hotspur*, which I had assumed would be my concluding visit to Carlisle. There were, however, a great many freight and parcel services still in the hands of steam and, with Kingmoor still available to service any visiting locomotives, several rail-tour organisations sought to exploit this situation by running specials over Shap and Ais Gill there.

Having initially held the opinion that rail tours were a 'cheating' way to travel behind steam locomotives, catching them working normal service trains being far more rewarding (and cheaper), I began to realise, at the beginning of 1966, that time was running out and the only way to obtain haulage by 'rare' locomotives was to travel on such trains. So, with the increased income generated by promotion within the clerical grades, I succumbed. It would seem similar views were shared by others within the haulage-bashing fraternity and it was on these trains that old acquaintances were renewed with information exchanged as to what had gone diesel, which classes of locomotives had become extinct, which sheds had closed etc. – in modern parlance getting 'genned up'.

So on the morning of Saturday 14 October 1967 I was to be found at Liverpool Exchange in order to join the Castle to Carlisle Rail Tour. This LCGB-organised tour ran, in an attempt to recuperate finances resulting from poor loadings, without the buffet car – thirst sated by a travelling trolley. Starting out of Liverpool Exchange at 09.15 with Speke Junction's BR 9F 92091 – probably the lure that enticed my patronage – the tour was routed via the Southport avoiding line, Wigan Wallgate and Chorley, eventually arriving into Preston from where the privately preserved GWR 7029 *Clun Castle* took over for the run north over Shap. Having then travelled over the goods lines, she was taken off our train at Rome Street Junction for servicing and turning at Kingmoor, whilst one of Kingmoor's Flying Pigs took the train forward the 15 miles along the Waverley route to the former Langholm branch junction station at Riddings Junction. It could have been one of many but as sure as eggs are eggs it had to be 43121 – one of two caught on a 'Nunex' into Keswick three months earlier! After running round, she returned us to the Citadel station via 'new' connection into the marshalling yard and the goods lines before running round again at Petteril Bridge Junction. *Clun Castle* then took us over Ais Gill, handing over to 92091 at Hellifield for the 66-mile run via myriad routes into Liverpool Lime Street at 20.57.

I had originally planned to return home after the above tour but, lured by the now rare Brit mileage available on a rail tour the following day, I phoned home before filling the night hours by travelling on the 01.00 sleepers portion from Manchester to Wigan prior to heading south to join the SLS-organised Carlisle Kingmoor tour on the Sunday morning at its starting point of Birmingham New Street. This tour, postponed from 24 September, utilised the subsequently preserved 70013 *Oliver Cromwell*; she faultlessly worked the 161 miles from Crewe to Kingmoor via Whalley and Ais Gill. Unlike my first outing to 12A, when a lot of shoe leather was used in getting there, this visit was far easier, being accessed off the rail tour. Hundreds of enthusiasts had alighted from the *Oliver Cromwell*-worked rail tour, the train being stabled, during the hour-long turnaround, adjacent to the running shed itself. I never did get to the Barry Island graveyard of steam; unlike at Dai Woodham's yard, here there was no future for the majority of occupants.

At the time of this visit the allocation was predictably dropping: a total of seventy-eight comprising just four classes: Black 5s (thirty six), 9Fs (twenty-four), Brits (sixteen) and Moguls (two). Having said that, with Kingmoor's obvious advantage of size, the shed had become a dumping ground and there were 108 locomotives on the site. As I wandered (without restriction) amongst them, climbing aboard, photographing them from all angles, it was with a sense of foreboding for the inevitable cessation of steam. Here was the undisputable proof that my all-embracing hobby, which had occupied my life for the last four years, was being taken away from me. Most of those machines witnessed that day had battled the gradients of Ais Gill, Shap and Beattock over the years – often with me aboard. It was so sad to observe them at the end of their lives awaiting the inevitable final fate of the cutter's torch. I had lived and breathed steam during my final teenage years: the need to chase and catch runs behind as many different steam locomotives had been prioritised over everything else. One by one the regions had dispensed with their need for the iron horse and now, after Kingmoor's closure, the remaining survivors were to be corralled at the north-west English depots within the Liverpool, Manchester and Carnforth triangle.

The DRB had even announced the dates: within ten months there would be no more British steam. I wasn't able to foresee that over half a century later, courtesy of the many hundreds of volunteers keeping well over 300 steam loco-motives going on both preserved and main lines, I would be able to continue to enjoy my hobby! I knew none of that back then. Here are the details of those 'cops' (all home depot-allocated unless otherwise shown):

In steam	44663 (9F), 44677, 44878, 44884, 44887, 44911, 45092 (10A), 45133 (8B), 45236, 45253, 45261 (9B), 45259, 45279, 45299 (6C), 45350 (8F), 45368 (8F), 45493, 48115 (9F), 48200 (9D), 48252 (9F), 48345 (9B), 48423 (10F), 70013 *Oliver Cromwell*, 70024 *Vulcan*, 70025 *Western Star*, 70049 *Solway Firth*, 92058, 92123 (6C), 92132, 92234 (6C)
Dead	44727, 44767, 44770, 44889 (10D), 44898, 44962 (8F), 45047 (9B), 45134, (10A) 45149 (10D), 45312 (9B), 45431 (8F), 48310 (10F), 48327 (9D), 48374 (8A), 48729 (9E), 70029 *Shooting Star*, 70035 *Rudyard Kipling*, 70045 *Lord Rowallan*, 92001 (6C), 92051, 92056, 92208, 92218
Works	45295, 70014 *Iron Duke*, 70022 *Tornado*
Withdrawn	42134 (12E), 43049, 43120, 43139, 44669, 44675, 44691 (12D), 44790, 44792, 44795, 44817, 44825, 44862, 44872 (10D), 44882, 44883, 44900, 44928, 44936, 44937, 45028, 45126, 45135, 45228, 45274, 45321 (8F), 45437, 45455, 45481, 48053 (10F), 48163 (8C), 48287 (5B), 70005 *John Milton*, 70010 *Owen Glendower*, 70015 *Apollo*, 70016 *Ariel*, 70028 *Royal Star*, 70032 *Tennyson*, 70033 *Charles Dickens*, 70037 *Hereward-the-Wake*, 70038 *Robin Hood*, 70039 *Sir Christopher Wren*, 70046 *Anzac*, 70047, 70052 *Firth of Tay*, 92014 (6C), 92052, 92074, 92114, 92119, 92139, 92204 (8C)

Because of delays on the returning train, I calculated that I could well have missed the last trains to my Kent home from London and so I alighted at Crewe and made yet another phone call back home. After assuring my parents all was well I travelled to Liverpool for the 23.38 York departure out of Lime Street, which that night was worked by one of Patricroft's Caprottis: 73136. Connecting, in the early hours of Monday, at Leeds into a St Pancras-bound train and having break-fasted at a cafe in Eversholt Street, Euston, I reported for work at Wimbledon in a somewhat dishevelled, unshaved state (I hadn't planned or equipped myself for being out for three nights). It was 'suggested' by my manager that a half-day's leave should be taken, to which I acquiesced, to protect my work colleagues' noses!

We now move on to Saturday 4 November 1967 and, having missed catch-ing a run on the 3-hour Glasgow–Aberdeen expresses with A4 60019 *Bittern*,

This photograph, together with the next twelve, was taken when visiting Kingmoor shed on Sunday 15 October 1967. Former Tebay Fairburn 2-6-4T 42134's onerous banking duties are forever over, she having been withdrawn in April 1967.

Long-term 12A resident snowplough-fitted Crewe-built 22-year-old Black 5 44884 is seen at rest. She 'escaped' to Newton Heath upon Kingmoor's closure that December, being withdrawn in June 1968 a month prior to that shed's closure.

Carnforth's 45092, caught by myself on the 'Belfast Boat Express' three months earlier, was visiting Kingmoor. She was withdrawn at the end of the year.

Having been withdrawn just eight days previously, 32-year-old Stanier 4-6-0 45135, with whom I travelled on a Barrow-bound service two months previously, awaits her inevitable destiny.

Armstrong Whitworth-built 45228, a 12A resident since May 1963, stands abandoned, having been withdrawn seven months previously.

Alive and kicking Heaton Mersey's North British-built 26-year-old, the first eight of which were in War Department stock, 8F 48252, with a further six months of existence ahead of her.

Here Brit 70010 *Owen Glendower*, a former ER, Willesden and Crewe locomotive reposes in the sun. Withdrawn the previous month, she had taken me over both Shap and Beattock banks in recent times.

The rail tour locomotive, 70013 *Oliver Cromwell*, having been turned to face south, is being watered and coaled for her return journey over Ais Gill. Upon closure of Kingmoor, she was the only Brit to survive, being transferred to Carnforth in order to work the plethora of specials during the final eight months. Being dispatched to Bressingham Museum after working the Fifteen Guinea Special in August 1968, she was returned to service and is a common performer today on both main and preserved lines.

70015 *Apollo* was one of three ex Stockport Brits initially placed in storage at Upperby. Although transferred to Kingmoor in June 1967, she was withdrawn (before I had a run with her) a mere two months later.

Once working prestige expresses out of Paddington, Brit 70028 *Royal Star*, having been transferred in from Crewe in September 1966, had been withdrawn four weeks previously.

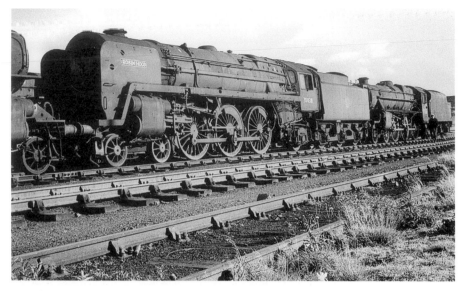

Transferred into Kingmoor in January 1964, the former ER-allocated Crewe-built Brit 70038 *Robin Hood* had also been withdrawn that August.

The elusive 14-year-old 70039 *Sir Christopher Wren* became my final required Brit. I eventually caught her out of Lancaster four weeks prior to her withdrawal in September 1967.

A long way from her Birkenhead home, 9-year-old Riddles-designed BR 9F 2-10-0 92234 was never to return, being withdrawn at Kingmoor that month.

it was a no brainer that I simply had to travel on this RCTS-organised A4 to Edinburgh rail tour. The other tick in the box this tour provided was a journey down the ECML into Scotland with steam, which I had not yet managed. *Bittern* was now privately preserved and was cleaned to perfection. Having completed the Calder Valley mail train bash in the dark early morning hours, I was now sufficiently awake to fully appreciate the spectacular coastal scenery being passed through as we followed the Northumberland coast, viewing Holy Island in the distance. This being my first daylight travel along the route, the obvious highlight was without doubt the crossing of the River Tweed on the twenty-eight-span 1850-built Royal Border Bridge.

There were mixed fortunes for Edinburgh's football clubs that day, with Heart of Midlothian beating Falkirk 1-0 but Hibernian losing 4-1 to Stirling.

Scotland itself was now, of course, steam free and so, after alighting from the tour, I made for the nearest steam locomotives −188 miles south at Preston! Brush Type 4 D1970 was the power for the Waverley-routed 15.00 stopper to Carlisle where, after enduring a further 90 DL miles over Shap, I finally returned to steam power in the form of the subsequently preserved Flying Pig 43106 on a Blackpool portion. The following day forty-nine persons perished in the Hither Green rail disaster (Bee Gee Robin Gibb was a survivor) and Henry Cooper was able to retain the Lonsdale belt by knocking out Billy Walker, leading to Cooper being crowned BBC Sports Personality of the Year.

The now preserved A4 60019 *Bittern* is seen being serviced at Edinburgh Waverley prior to returning to Leeds with a rail tour on Saturday 4 November 1967. She had been one of the final 3 A4s on the 3-hour Glasgow–Aberdeen expresses, being withdrawn in October 1966. (Keith Lawrence)

Isolated steam-powered penetrations continued on the 09.20 and 19.44 Waverley route and 20.32 Beattock route departures out of Carlisle during the final three months of Kingmoor's existence. On the G&SWR route steam locomotives were being taken off at Kilmarnock – an example being on 7 December (70028) while working a control-organised relief train due to a disruption to passenger services by a derailment in England. On 14 December 70024 *Vulcan* worked through to Glasgow Sighthill with a Christmas parcels extra and on the 30th 70004 worked to Kilmarnock with the 03.08 Carlisle–Ayr mails. During 12A's final month, December 1967, just forty-five locomotives remained, comprising Black 5s (twenty-two), Brits (fourteen) and 9Fs (nine).

Following the closure of the yard and depot, wildlife began to recolonise the area before it was opened as a nature reserve in 1987. Carlisle City Council has allowed the location to become the Sidings Nature Reserve and, although I have never visited it, I understand relics of the site's past glory are discernable amongst the undergrowth. The leaf litter from the dense silver birch woodland, grown from seed blown in over the years, has improved the soil and led to other trees such as oak and ash taking up residence. The nutrient-poor soils of Kingmoor Sidings, in particular heaps of ash, are also home to a wide variety of wildflower species, including wild orchids, vetches and birdsfoot trefoils. There is usually a year-round display of fungi, with everything from the poisonous yet colourful fly agarics to the less colourful birch polypore on display. There are picnic benches and resting places throughout the reserve. The footpaths do get muddy and slippery in places, so good walking boots are a must, as are pocket-sized field guides to plants and birds so that you can enjoy all that the Kingmoor Sidings Nature Reserve has to offer.

To the best of my knowledge (and I am prepared to be corrected) only three Brits worked trains in 1968. The February 1968 issue of *The Railway World* reported 70045 *Lord Rowallan* working forward from Carlisle to Glasgow in the early hours of January with a Hogmanay special originating from Manchester. Was that true, taking into consideration the ScR's ban on steam into Glasgow which was operative during the back end of 1967? Was it even the correct loco-motive number, because irrefutable photographic evidence in a *Steam Railway* magazine (2010) shows the same Brit, having worked a 13.10 Carlisle–Skipton freight on the 30th, at Rose Grove shed on 31 December – she being sent out to work a Rose Grove–Wigan coal train in the early hours of 1968. Then, of course, 70013 *Oliver Cromwell* was reallocated to Carnforth and, having worked many rail tours, including the (unaffordable to a lowly paid railway clerk) Fifteen Guinea Special, she headed off to East Anglia and into preservation.

Summing it all up, Scotland had provided me with runs behind seven never caught before, different classes of steam locomotives for which I was truly grateful: visiting Britannias, Clans and a Jubilee, together with a resident A2, V2, several A4s and B1s. I have never regretted those wonderful teenage years spent chasing steam throughout Britain – so often remembered by articles in steam-orientated magazines (to which I occasionally contribute). I hope the foregoing has either brought back many memories for those readers present at the time or, for youngsters, created a picture of those halcyon days of Scottish steam.

17

MANY HAPPY RETURNS

APPRECIATING MOST READERS will have anticipated the contents of this book as being perhaps purely of steam train travels, can I enact my writer's licence in relating some further visits to Scotland – post steam? Although the hectic five years of steam chasing, four in the UK and one in Europe, were behind me, any long-term railway enthusiast will agree that, even though the urgency and reasoning behind all those travels had dissipated, travelling still remains in the blood – perhaps on a less frenetic basis. It would have been sacrilege not to use the free and reduced-rate ticket concessions afforded to me for being an employee of BR, and so contained within this final chapter are some brief outlines of my further exploits across the border.

With my lifelong friends Graham 'Jock' Aitken (who spent his formative years in the Edinburgh suburb of Eskbank) and Owen 'Blodders' Davies, upon the announcement concerning the closure of the Waverley route in 1969, one final visit to the line just had to be made. Saturday 4 January saw us depart Euston and, changing at Carlisle on to a Peak-hauled (Class 45) train, headed for Hawick, staying there at a prearranged B&B – sampling, in my case for the very first time, haggis while hitting the night life that evening. On the Sunday morning we headed to Edinburgh by bus (the only Sunday train on the route being that night's southbound sleeper service), calling in at a pub in Eskbank and visiting (by foot) the recently (1964) opened Forth Road Bridge prior to boarding the very last train over the Waverley Line.

This was 1M82 21.56 Edinburgh Waverley–London St Pancras sleeper on Sunday 5 January 1969, hauled by Class 45 Peak D60 *Lytham St Annes*. Feelings were running high amongst the local populace during that final weekend of

Hawick platform ticket, recently discovered in the author's attic.

passenger operations, with protesters evident at most stations, and the authorities, sensing the potential for trouble, sent a Clayton DL ahead of 1M82 under caution from Hawick to 'prove' the route south after a set of points at Whitrope were found to have been tampered with. At Newcastleton the pilot engine found the line was blocked and the level crossing gates locked by protesters, led by the parish minister, the Reverend Brydon Maben. When a young police officer was sent to arrest him it turned out that he was the reverend's son! Maben Jr dutifully marched his father off to the police station and David Steel MP was summoned from his bed (aboard the train) by the guard and was persuaded to address the crowd from the footbridge. Steel made an agreement with the crowd that if the police released the minister the crowd would allow the train through. They did and the train continued its journey 2 hours late. Later that morning the line manager at our place of work had, once again, listened with incredulity to yet another reason for our late arrivals – they being eventually collaborated by that evening's news on the television.[*]

In August that same year the same three intrepid explorers travelled, having undertaken a car-orientated holiday to south-west and central Scotland, on the Motorail south out of Perth for Kensington with, unlike previous departures for London a few years earlier with either a Black 5 or a Clan, a Brush Type 4.

I had always kept a BR map of the system marked as to which lines I had travelled over and, now that steam had finished, there were some major

---

[*] It should be noted at this point that Jock returned on 6 September 2015 to travel on the very first train from Edinburgh to Tweedbank, and was interviewed by BBC Scotland to boot.

On 30 September 1971 Sulzer Type 2 5332 (Class 26) awaits time at Kyle of Lochalsh (without the Skye Road Bridge disfiguring the scene) with the 17.50 for Inverness.

The following day and sister 5343 is at Wick with an evening Inverness departure.

Thurso on 2 October 1971 and Type 2 5132 (Class 24) is seen with the 11.25 portion for Georgemas Junction.

omissions of diesel-operated lines to 'colour in'. January 1970 saw the Oban route cleared on a flying overnight visit ostensibly because the Scottish sleepers travelled via the required track, subsequently closed completely eleven years later, of the Northampton–Market Harborough line.

Moving on to September 1971 and, with impending domesticity beckoning, one final three-day 'freedom' trip was made (inevitably with Jock) resulting in marking off the Mallaig, Kyle of Lochalsh, Wick and Thurso branches – all loco hauled, of course. There was still one major line remaining to be covered: that between Inverness and Aberdeen via my namesake's town of Keith. Taking advantage of my by then Crewe-based residency, this was resolved in December 1975 by staying overnight in Aberdeen and returning south over a snow-covered Beattock in a vehicle whose lights had failed. The white panoramic outside scenes were wonderfully accentuated by the adjacent vehicle's illuminations and the arcing from the overhead wires.

The opportunity arose, during the mid–late 1980s for explorations further afield and in August 1986 the Outer Hebrides were eliminated from my 'haven't been there yet' map. Ever the haulage basher, while staying at Inverness one evening several ETH-equipped Class 37s were scratched on an evening outing to Dingwall – whilst the remainder of the party went drinking! Finally the Inner Hebrides were visited in August 1987 – the highlight of that trip being a

With Ben Nevis in the background, English Electric (Class 37) Type 3 37408 *Lord Rannoch* awaits time at Fort William with the 17.40 Euston-bound sleepers on 30 August 1987.

Withdrawn at Lostock Hall in August 1968, the now Great Central Railway-based 50-year-old Black 5 45305 *Alderman A.E. Draper* departs Mallaig with a Fort William service on 30 August 1987.

Another survivor is BR-built K1 2-6-0 62005. She is the very last steam locomotive to be withdrawn on the former North Eastern Region of BR (at Leeds Holbeck in November 1967) and is currently based at the North Yorkshire Moors Railway. Here she is seen at Mallaig on 30 August 1987 with a Fort William service.

The view of the Glenfinnan Viaduct from the above train.

run with steam in Scotland once more. Although having already encountered the locomotive concerned, LNER K1 2-6-0 62005, twenty years previously on a Yorkshire Dales rail tour, the Mallaig–Fort William journey I undertook that warm August evening through the breathtakingly scenic Scottish landscape perhaps reignited my somewhat dormant interest in chasing steam. Nowadays, when aware of a required locomotive within easy catching distance from my home (i.e. no overnights!), I kick-start my weary bones into action and once again relive the enthusiasm associated with redlining entries in my self-fashioned list of preserved icons.

Caledonian Railway 2P 0-4-4T 55189 is seen a long way from her then Falkirk home when visiting the Bluebell Railway in August 1982. Constructed at St Rollox in 1907, this McIntosh-designed locomotive was one of a ninety-two-strong class and became one of the final four, being withdrawn at Carstairs in December 1962. Owned by the SRPS, she is currently based at Bo'ness & Kinneil Railway.

AN AFTERTHOUGHT

STEAM ON SCOTTISH main lines has enjoyed a romantic renaissance with regular timetabled Jacobite trains over the West Highland Line Mallaig extension. Other steam specials in Scotland are less frequent but no less spectacular. Every year multi-day steam specials such as The Great Britain and Cathedrals Explorer run over scenic routes. The SRPS also runs tours using its own rake of Mark 1s, including its Forth Circle trips often using a K1 or an A4, and of course the recently reopened Waverley route now regularly witnesses steam workings.

I consider myself fortunate in being the age I am. As a teenager in the 1960s, the demise of steam ran parallel with the freedom parents often allowed their offspring back then. Frequently not seeing me from the Friday morning until the Sunday lunchtime, they never expressed any worries or concerns in regard to my safety, secure in the knowledge that I was enjoying the risk-adverse hobby of, in their words, trainspotting. Although, as a BR clerk, my pay wasn't substantial, by utilising the travel perks associated with the job Britain's then extensive network was at my mercy – and boy did I make the most of them. The thrill of the chase – that of travelling behind as many different locomotives as possible prior to their annihilation – can only be compared to that of an adrenaline junkie. Friendly rivalry abounded. The reward for our efforts was a red-lined entry in our *Locoshed* books. Even that didn't last long – being usually obliterated within months, as the prey caught was withdrawn. If I was ever stranded on a desert island and was given a choice of taking one item with me I would take my attaché case crammed full of notebooks and ABCs so I could relive those glorious years.

Gresley-designed D49 4-4-0 62712 *Morayshire*, built at Darlington in 1928, is the only survivor of the once seventy-six-strong class. Also based at the Bo'ness Railway, she had been withdrawn at Hawick in June 1961 and, as part of a countrywide tour during early 2015, is seen here at Weybourne participating in the North Norfolk Railway's Spring Gala.

Fast forward to the present day and against all odds my hobby can still be enjoyed courtesy of an amazing bunch of stalwart enthusiasts whom, over the years, have salvaged upwards of 300 steam locomotives from beyond the grave. Their efforts, the results of which can regularly be viewed on both main and preserved lines, are a joy to behold: steam galas, Thomas the Tank events, anniversary celebrations – irrespective of the reasons, thousands of people come out to pay homage to the 'relics' of Britain's industrial past. With over seventy steam locomotives requiring my attendance on a train behind them, it seems my hobby remains secure. My present stats are 1,251 locomotives for 101,214 miles – how are yours?

APPENDIX 1

STEAM LOCOMOTIVE WHEEL ARRANGEMENTS

0–6–0	
0–8–0	
2–6–0	First figure indicates number of leading wheels
2–6–2	
2–6–4	Second figure indicates number of powered and coupled driving wheels
2–8–0	
2–10–0	Third figure indicates number of trailing wheels
4–6–0	
4–6–2	

INDEX OF ALL STEAM JOURNEYS MADE ON SCOTTISH REGION METALS

1965					
	Locomotive	**Shed**	**Train**	**Miles**	**Remarks**
Saturday 29 May	45012	12A	02.09 Carlisle–Stranraer Harbour ('The Northern Irishman')	106¾	19.30 ex Euston
	45467	67E	03.13 Dumfries–Castle Douglas	19¾	Assisted
	70005	12A	15.01 Carstairs–Stirling	44	09.25 Crewe–Perth
	60034	61B	16.45 Stirling–Glasgow Buchanan Street ('The Grampian')	30¼	13.30 ex Aberdeen
	73151	65B	17.35 Glasgow Buchanan Street–Larbert	22	For Dunblane
Saturday 24 July	70002	12A	02.09 Carlisle–Dumfries ('The Northern Irishman')	32¾	19.30 Euston–Stranraer
	45259	12A	04.14 Dumfries–Kilmarnock	58¼	03.21 Carlisle–Ayr
	80111	67A	05.51 Kilmarnock–Troon	9	
	73102	67A	08.09 Kilmarnock–Glasgow St Enoch	24¼	06.10 ex Annan
	60007	61B	15.50 Perth–Glasgow Buchanan Street ('The Grampian')	63¼	13.30 ex Aberdeen

	73150	65B	18.15 Glasgow Buchanan Street–Perth	63¼	For Dundee
	72008	12A	20.25 Perth–Carstairs	77	For Marylebone
Saturday 7 August	70033	12A	02.xx Carlisle–Perth	150½	22.35 ex Manch Ex
	60026	61B	11.05 Dundee Tay Bridge–Edinburgh Waverley	59¼	09.10 ex Aberdeen
	61133	62A	13.18 Edinburgh Waverley–Inverkeithing	13¼	For Crail
	61343	62A	14.07 Inverkeithing–Edinburgh Waverley	13¼	12.30 ex Crail
	60009	61B	18.09 Stirling–Perth	33	17.30 Glasgow Buchanan Street–Aberdeen
	45120	12A	20.25 Perth–Carstairs	77	For Marylebone
	45593	55A	23.24 Carstairs–Carlisle	73½	
Saturday 21 August	44802	12A	01.xx Carlisle–Carstairs	73½	19.02 Euston–Inverness
	45126	12A	03.xx Carstairs–Perth	77	
	60024	64A	10.34 Arbroath–Leuchars Junction	25½	09.10 Aberdeen–Edinburgh Waverley
	44704	63A	11.56 Leuchars Junction–Dundee Tay Bridge	8½	10.30 Edinburgh Waverley–Aberdeen
	45390	10A	14.00 Dundee Tay Bridge–Perth	20¾	For Glasgow Buchanan Street
	73153	65B	18.12 Larbert–Stirling	8¼	17.35 Glasgow Buchanan Street–Dunblane
	60528	62B	19.03 Stirling–Perth	33	18.15 Glasgow Buchanan Street–Dundee

	Locomotive	Shed	Train	Miles	Remarks
	44672	12A	20.26 Perth–Carlisle	11	101 Marylebone
	72007	12A	23.24 Carstairs–Carlisle	73½	
1966					
Saturday 4 June	70004	9B	Liverpool Lime Street–Quintinshill	135½	
	44767	12A	Carnforth–Quintinshill	73	Assisted
	45593	55A	Quintinshill–Crewe	169½	Rail Tour
	45596	9B	Quintinshill–Crewe	169½	
Friday 1 July	70033	12A	16.35 Carlisle–Carstairs	73½	13.27 Liverpool–Glasgow Central
	42274	66E	Beattock bank	10	Assisted
	45127	64A	18.16 Carstairs–Edinburgh Waverley	29	
	44703	61B	22.42 Kirkcaldy–Edinburgh Waverley	26	19.45 Aberdeen–York
Saturday 9 July	45593	55A	02.25 Leeds City–Glasgow Central	229½	21.20 ex St Pancras
	60024	61B	08.25 Glasgow Buchanan Street–Stirling ('The Grampian')	30¼	For Aberdeen
	45168	64A	11.19 Dunfermline Lower–Perth	31	10.45 Edinburgh Waverley–Inverness
	73149	65B	12.39 Perth–Dundee Tay Bridge	20¾	11.00 ex Glasgow Buchanan Street
	61263	62B	13.20 Dundee Tay Bridge–Aberdeen	71¼	
	60024	61B	17.15 Aberdeen–Glasgow Buchanan Street ('The Granite City')	153	
	70017	12A	23.46 Ayr–Carlisle ('The Northern Irishman')	90½	22.10 Stranraer Harbour–Euston
Saturday 6 August	70006	12A	20.25 Carlisle–Coatbridge Central	94¼	For Perth

Saturday 13 August	70006	12A	03.xx Carlisle–Glasgow Central	102½	21.50 ex Euston
	76098	66F	Beattock bank	10	Assisted
	60813	62B	10.32 Inverkeithing–Edinburgh Waverley	13¼	09.10 Dundee–Blackpool North
	73108	66E	11.25 Edinburgh Waverley–Carstairs	27¾	For Liverpool–Manchester
	45445	10A	12.13 Carstairs–Glasgow Central	29	08.20 ex Morecambe
	45490 45227	67B 10A	13.25 Glasgow Central–Carlisle	116½	For Morecambe
Friday 19 August	44989	12A	16.35 Carlisle–Carstairs	73½	13.27 Liverpool–Glasgow Central
	80111	66F	Beattock bank	10	Assisted
	44997	63A	22.42 Kirkcaldy–Edinburgh Waverley	26	19.45 ex Aberdeen
Friday 16 September	70009	12A	02.22 Carlisle–Stranraer Harbour ('The Northern Irishman')	149½	20.40 ex Euston
	45423	67C	04.25 Ayr–Stranraer Harbour	59	Assisted
	73079	67A	12.18 Glasgow Central–Ayr	40½	
	70005	12A	20.25 Carlisle–Carstairs	73½	For Perth

1967

	Locomotive	Shed	Train	Miles	Remarks
Saturday 15 April	70010	12A	20.32 Carlisle–Carstairs	73½	For Perth
Friday 28 April	44699	67A	06.55 Glasgow Central–Hillington West	5	
	80004	67A	07.34 Hillington West–Renfrew Wharf	5	07.19 ex Glasgow Central
	70022	12A	20.32 Carlisle–Carstairs	73½	For Perth
Saturday 29 April	70012	12A	21.10 Carlisle–Carstairs	73½	For Perth
Saturday 20 May	70023	12A	20.32 Carlisle–Carstairs	73½	For Perth
Friday 26 May	70016	12A	03.xx Carlisle–Glasgow Central	102½	22.07 ex Euston
	44795	12A	18.xx Carlisle–Lockerbie	25¾	12.10 Euston–Perth

	44674	12A	20.22 Carlisle–Coatbridge Central	94¼	For Perth
Saturday 27 May	70038	12A	16.33 Carlisle–Glasgow Central	116½	09.20 ex St Pancras
	70010	12A	22.32 Carstairs–Coatbridge Central	21¼	20.32 Carlisle–Perth
Monday 29 May	70038	12A	20.32 Carlisle–Coatbridge Central	94¼	For Perth
Sunday 16 July	70024	12A	04.50 Carlisle–Glasgow Central	126¾	21.20 ex St Pancras
Saturday 22 July	70021	12A	13.30 Carlisle–Dumfries	32¾	06.40 Birmingham–Glasgow Central
Friday 28 July	45455	12A	17.48 Carlisle–Motherwell	89¾	12.10 Euston–Perth
Friday 11 August	70032	12A	19.xx Carlisle–Glasgow Control	116½	13.52 ex Euston
Saturday 14 October	43121	12A	Carlisle–Riddings Junction	15¼	Rail Tour
	43121	12A	Riddings Junction–Carlisle	18¾	
Saturday 4 November	60019	PRES	08.45 Leeds City–Edinburgh Waverley	230¼	Rail Tour
1987					
	Locomotive	**Shed**	**Train**	**Miles**	**Remarks**
Sunday 30 August	62005	PRES	Mallaig–Fort William	41½	Adex

APPENDIX 3

STEAM SHEDS WITHIN THE SCOTTISH REGION OF BR

Date	Shed closed to steam	Running total
May 1965		24
October 1965	64C Dalry Road, 65C Parkhead	22
November 1965	65F Grangemouth	21
January 1966	64G Hawick	20
November 1966	65A Eastfield (Glasgow), 65B St Rollox, 67E Dumfries	17
December 1966	64F Bathgate, 66D Greenock (Ladyburn), 66E Carstairs, 65J Stirling, 67B Hurlford, 67C Ayr, 67F Stranraer	10
February 1967	64A St Margarets (Edinburgh)	9
March 1967	61B Aberdeen (Ferryhill)	8
April 1967	62A Thornton Junction, 66F Beattock	6
May 1967	62B Dundee (Tay Bridge), 62C Dunfermline, 63A Perth, 66A Polmadie (Glasgow), 66B Motherwell, 67A Corkerhill (Glasgow)	0

APPENDIX 4

STEAM ALLOCATIONS WITHIN THE SCOTTISH REGION OF BR

Origin	Power	Wheels	Design	May 1965	Sep 1965	Jan 1966	May 1966	Sep 1966	Jan 1967	Apr 1967	May 1967
LMS	4MT	2-6-4T	Fairburn	26	22	17	14	5	1	1	–
LMS	5MT	2-6-0	Hughes	21	18	16	13	7	–	–	–
LMS	5MT	4-6-0	Stanier	113	93	84	79	51	13	9	–
LMS	2MT	2-6-0	Ivatt	11	8	6	4	1	–	–	–
LNER	8P (A4)	4-6-2	Gresley	10	8	6	5	2	–	–	–
LNER	7P (A3)	4-6-2	Gresley	3	2	1	–	–	–	–	–
LNER	7MT (A2)	4-6-2	Peppercorn	6	3	3	3	2	–	–	–
LNER	6MT (V2)	2-6-2	Gresley	13	12	9	7	1	–	–	–
LNER	5MT (B1)	4-6-0	Thompson	45	38	32	31	19	9	2	–
NBR	5F (J37)	0-6-0	Reid	24	21	17	14	9	4	–	–
NBR	2F (J36)	0-6-0	Holmes	9	9	8	6	5	3	2	2*
LNER	6F (J38)	0-6-0	Gresley	23	22	21	20	15	3	–	–
BR	5MT	4-6-0	Riddles	41	34	29	25	14	5	5	–
BR	4MT	2-6-0	Riddles	37	35	33	27	19	6	5	–
BR	3MT	2-6-0	Riddles	10	10	10	8	5	–	–	–
BR	2MT	2-6-0	Riddles	10	10	9	6	3	–	–	–
BR	4MT	2-6-4T	Riddles	47	45	42	40	19	8	6	–
BR	8F	2-8-0	Riddles	24	23	21	21	15	7	–	–
			Total	473	413	364	323	192	59	30	2*

★ J36s 65288 (62C) and 65345 (62A) withdrawn on 5 June 1967

APPENDIX 5

LINES OR STATIONS CLOSED (TO PASSENGERS) TRAVELLED OVER

Route	Visited	Closure
Dumfries–Stranraer	May 1965	June 1965
Edinburgh Princes Street	May 1965	September 1965
Leven–St Andrews	July 1965	September 1965
Glasgow St Enoch	July 1965	June 1966
Glasgow Buchanan Street	July 1966	November 66
Paisley–Renfrew Wharf	April 1967	June 1967
Alloa–Larbert	August 1965	January 1968
Dunfermline–Alloa–Stirling	August 1965	October 1968(a)
Edinburgh–Hawick–Carlisle	January 1969	January 1969(b)
St Andrews–Leuchars Junction	July 1965	January 1969
Wormit–Tayport	August 1965	May 1969
Thornton Junction–Leven	July 1965	October 1969
Perth–Kinross–Cowdenbeath	July 1966	January 1970
Kilmarnock–Dalry	July 1967	October 1973

(a) Alloa–Stirling reopened May 2008

(b) Edinburgh–Tweedbank reopened September 2015

APPENDIX 6

PRESERVED RAILWAYS IN SCOTLAND

Please visit these railways and support the efforts of the volunteers who will-ingly give their time to recreate the steam railway lost in the 1960s. Without them the heritage industry would be that much poorer and future generations would never be able to participate and enjoy the pleasures of steam train travel: Alford Valley Railway, Almond Valley Light Railway, Bo'ness & Kinneil Railway, Caledonian Railway (Brechin), Keith & Dufftown Railway, Leadhills & Wanlockhead Railway, Ness Islands Railway, Royal Deeside Railway, Scottish Industrial Railway Centre, Strathspey Railway.

GLOSSARY OF TERMS

Adex	Advertised excursion
BR	British Rail(ways) (1948–97)
BRB	British Rail Board
BSK	Brake standard corridor
CR	Caledonian Railway (Caley) (1845–1922)
CWR	Continuous welded rail
DL	Diesel locomotive
DMO	Divisional manager's office
DMU	Diesel (mechanical) multiple unit
DSL	Diesel shunting locomotive
ECML	East Coast Main Line (King's Cross to Edinburgh via York)
ECS	Empty coaching stock
E&GR	Edinburgh & Glasgow Railway (1838–65)
EL	Electric locomotive
ER	Eastern Region of BR (1948–92)
EMU	Electric multiple unit
ETH	Electric train heating
F	Power ratio for freight traffic
FO	Fridays only
Footex	Advertised excursions run in connection with a football event
FSO	Fridays and Saturdays only
G&SWR	Glasgow & South Western Railway (1850–1922)
GCR	Great Central Railway (1897–1922)
GWML	Great Western Main Line

GWR	Great Western Railway (1835–1947)
LE	Light engine
LCGB	The Locomotive Club of Great Britain
LMR	London Midland Region of BR (1948–92)
LMS	London Midland & Scottish Railway (1923–47)
LNER	London & North Eastern Railway (1923–47)
L&NWR	London & North Western Railway (1846–1922)
L&SWR	London & South Western Railway (1838–1922)
MNA	Master Neverers Association – a group of enthusiasts who travelled the country purely to externally clean (usually overnight) steam locomotives working the 'final' or 'last' services, to the benefit of photographers. The word 'neverer' meant that there was never any intention of them paying any fares when travelling by train to or from their selected subject.
Mogul	Locomotive wheel arrangement (2-6-0)
MP	Milepost
MR	Midland Railway (1844–1922)
MT	Mixed traffic (passenger and freight)
MX	Mondays excepted (Tuesdays to Saturdays)
NBR	North British Railway (1844–1922)
NER	North Eastern Region (1923–47)
NRM	National Rail Museum
Nunex	A Keswick convention special
P	Power ratio for passenger traffic
Pacific	Locomotive wheel arrangement (4-6-2)
Parspec	Advertised excursions run for private parties
RCTS	The Railway Correspondence & Travel Society
S&D	Somerset & Dorset Railway (1862–1922)
ScR	Scottish Region of BR (1948–92)
SLS	The Stephenson Locomotive Society
SO	Saturdays only
SR	Southern Region of BR (1948–92)
STN	Special traffic notice
SX	Saturdays excepted (Mondays to Fridays)
T	Tank
TMD	Traction maintenance depot
WCML	West Coast Main Line (Euston to Glasgow via Crewe)
WD	War Department
WR	Western Region of BR (1948–92)

SOURCES

BR Database

Hugh Longworth, 'BR Steam Locomotives 1948–1968': Six Bells Junction
    website

Ian Allan 1966 Trains Annual

The Engine Shed Society, BR Steam Locomotive sheds and allocations

The LCGB monthly bulletin

The Railway World magazine

To view my website please go to mistermixedtraction.smugmug.com and then
select one of twenty galleries, 'Scotland' being particularly relevant to this book.
Simply click on 'slideshow', sit back and enjoy. Anyone wishing to purchase
copies of the images contained here please visit www.railwayimages.com and
by typing 'Widdowson' in the search box you can access my photographs of
the final five years of BR steam.

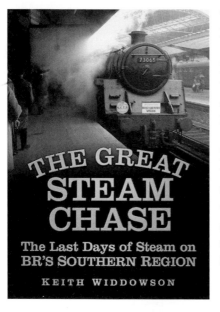

**Riding Yorkshire's Final Steam Trains,
Keith Widdowson,** 978 0 7509 6047 2

Review by *Heritage Railway Magazine*
'Capturing the mid-1960s atmosphere well
remembered by many enthusiasts, this is a
well-written and entertaining book, illus-
trated with many black and white pictures
of steam in Yorkshire's West Riding.'

Review by *Today's Railways Magazine*
'This tale is an elegiac evocation of a
bygone age and bygone pleasures, which
will awaken memories in many readers.'

Review by *Steam Railway Magazine*
'An excellent book.'

**The Great Steam Chase,
Keith Widdowson,** 978 0 7524 7957 6

Review by *Steam Railway Magazine*
'A well-written, valuable glimpse of one
of the most important periods of railway
history.'

Review by Railwayimages.com
'If you were alive in the 60s and followed
the last years of SR steam this superb book
will bring it all back. If you were too young
get a copy and wallow in the excitement
and nostalgia of those final days of steam.
Superb illustrations and detailed memories.'

The
History
Press

The destination for history
www.thehistorypress.co.uk

Oth

Child N

Advance ig

Whaley a dren's Nursing (199?) with Steph

Camp P atric Ambulatory Care (1998) (with

Innovatio

Susan

Contents